MW00437624

MOONLIGHT 'PON WIRE

memoirs of a spiritual journey

YASMINE ANNE FERNANDEZ

Dedication

This book is dedicated to all my teachers physically and spiritually. To all of nature, tuning in to your rhythm allowed me to find my own and recognize that all is connected.

Cover Design & Book Layout
By
Raymond Fernandez
raymond-fernandez.squarespace.com

In support of music and the arts...
ottarts.org

Acknowledgments

A special thank you to my children Lana and Ray. You are not only my children but also my best friends. To my grandchildren Briana and Mia, you remind me to participate in life and see everything with new eyes. Paul and Rhonda, my stepchildren, thank you for sharing a part of this journey with me. To those who challenged me in opposition, you presented me with opportunities that helped me grow.

Thank you, and a big hug to my friend Donna Phillips for her ongoing support and assistance with copy editing.

To my friends Sharon Donaldson, Danielle Watson and Lynn Klopfer, I appreciate your support and encouragement throughout the process.

Thank you, Greg, for reminding me about "moonlight 'pon wire," and to Luis, for his dedication and help with printing.

Introduction

This story is about my own physical and spiritual journey that began with a less complex life, where a smile went a long way and a connection with nature catapulted me onto a spiritual path. My life experiences are vast with many trials and tribulations, but my connection with the spirit world and other dimensions is the one thread woven through the tapestry of my life, that kept me from falling off the edge into the dark abyss.

I have come full circle, now as a grandmother in the final phase of this physical life. I am drawn to a simple lifestyle, and my connection with nature is heightened. My spiritual path moves me into many dimensions connecting with guides who assist me on my life's journey and work through me to help others. Even though I walk many paths in this lifetime, I have come to the realization that every single step, every experience happened for a reason.

Everything and everyone is connected. We are born into this world with a fully equipped hard drive and all that we need to help us on our individual journey. It is through the process of life that we begin to recall, step by step, what we already knew from the beginning. Spiritual growth and a sense of humor have kept me sane on this journey. I have learned to laugh at myself.

My one consistent goal, spiritual enlightenment, brings me

to this place on my journey, with joy, love and compassion, knowing that "going home" is to be celebrated, because there is no beginning and no end. I may possibly be coming full circle again. The timing is right, and I hope that through reading about my experiences, others can feel more at ease, knowing there are millions of people breaking through the barriers of old beliefs to reach their higher paths.

Currently, many people are feeling tested. Much friction and unrest are occurring on the planet. This is an opportunity for growth. Pay attention to your journey, polish your skills and be ready for the next shift in consciousness.

We are moving into another Golden Age.

Author's house in Trinidad

Contents

Part 1

Village Life

"Oh me God, the sky opening up!"

I walked outside onto the village street to see my neighbors staring up into the sky - at a line that went all the way across. It looked like the sky would open up at any moment, and we were very concerned. We all went back to our daily routines, still in wonderment as the line faded from the sky.

I have always had two clearly distinct personalities. As a young girl growing up in a small village on the island of Trinidad, I would lead my many friends on adventures that would sometimes cause the intervention of parents and/or neighbors, threatening some form of punishment. I would set out to do the very things I was told not to do. I had to see for myself. I had to step out into the unknown.

Fearlessly, I pulled myself across the branch of the tamarind tree hanging over the swift moving river that had already claimed the lives of three children. My friends shouted in Trinidad lingo, "Why you doh pick the tamarinds way it safer?" I was always testing the waters.

One of my neighbors saw me just in time, as the branch lowered into the river, and screamed, "Get dong from dey or I go call your muddah!" It was the only threat that could stop me in my path. Mother made the rules and when they were broken, she followed through mostly with a "talking to" that was worse than a spanking. "Sheba if you know wah good for you, you go get yo little ass over here now." These words, spoken in West Indian lingo by my mother, became her mantra. Sheba was my nickname.

On other occasions I would lead my playmates down to

the river. Their apprehension that the alligator might be there, and words that expressed fear, caused me to be more determined to jump in the water. They stood on the river banks and as I splashed around I kept an eye on the alligator. I would wait until he entered the water before making my way out. The one comment from my friends that stood out amongst others was "you crazy gyal."

My mother was born in England of English and French descent. Since her family was financially stable, at age eighteen she was able to travel to Trinidad with her mother for vacation. Trinidad and Tobago were under British rule at the time, and this made it easy for English folks to escape the dreary weather in England and spend time on this diverse tropical island.

Trinidad and its sister island, Tobago, are situated above Venezuela in the Caribbean Sea. The white sand beaches are filled with coconut and palm trees, and the warm tropical waters reflect the blue sky, luring you in to immerse yourself in tranquility.

Trinidad citizens are the most eclectic of all the Caribbean island natives, mixed with Black, Indian, Spanish, Chinese, English and French. With parents from Pakistan, my father was born in Trinidad, where his family lived a life of poverty working in the sugar cane fields.

One of the many jobs my father had was driving a taxi in the town called Port of Spain. The story, told to me by my parents, was that my mother hailed a taxi that happened to be my father's and after that encounter, my mother never left Trinidad. She married my father, and her family disowned her because she married a man who was Indian and very poor.

They settled in a small village called Caroni, surrounded by sugar cane fields with a river running through it. Most of the streets were paved with dirt. Most of the homes were constructed from wood, and some had walls built from cow dung and mud brought up from the river.

Fruit trees, such as mango, banana and plum, were abundant. Coconut trees provided us with food, oil, soap and mattresses, which were made with the dried fiber from the shell (one of my many chores). I would gather the dried coconuts, cut them in half with a cutlass, pull the dried fiber apart, wash it and then lay it out to dry. The shell could be used as a bowl, and the coconut for food and other products.

Once a week I would scrub the dilapidated wooden floors in our home with a scrub brush and bucket of water...on my knees. When laundry overflowed from the basket, I would help my mother wash our clothes in a wooden tub with a scrubbing board.

My mother adjusted very quickly to the Trinidad culture and lifestyle. Five kids later, she had lost her English accent and spoke just like the locals with their West Indian slang. The villagers, who were mostly Indians and Blacks, addressed her as "the white lady" - she was the only white person in the village.

I yearned to be alone in nature and allow the quiet to set my mind free. I would often run through the sugar cane fields and find myself an open spot. Surrounded by the cane stalks, I would lie on my back and stare up at the sky, feeling at peace.

The excitement I felt about climbing to the top of the plum tree in my yard and looking out at the vastness of the sugar cane fields was sometimes overwhelming. As soon as I came home from school, I would quickly finish my chores and then climb to the highest part of the tree. There was a connection from the moment I placed my bare hands and feet on the limbs of the tree, and at the very top, I would drift off to a place that embraced me in a blanket of warmth and love.

There was a vast nothingness, and it was here that I would have a knowing about my life and things to come. There was much more to the journey than I was currently experiencing - it was a knowing deep within. This place felt like my home. I belonged. The experience caused me to smile often, and a sense of joy and peace would rise up from deep inside me. I didn't quite understand why, but it did not matter.

These two personalities have always been and are still present in my life today. I genuinely love and enjoy people and socializing, but I must be alone in nature to rejuvenate my body and soul and connect with my spiritual home.

Author at 4 years old with brother

"Sheba, Sheba"

Late one night with the whole family asleep, except for my father who worked the night shifts on an oil barge as a radio operator, I was awakened by a quiet whisper in my ear. "Sheba, Sheba." (My father had nicknamed me "Sheba" at birth, because I was his first born, and he had just seen the movie Queen of Sheba.)

I was only seven years old, sleeping in the same room with my mother and my four siblings. Our house was small and built from dirt and cow dung, with a corrugated aluminum roof. Poverty and practicality were the reasons for the materials used in building our home. It was strong enough to keep out the weather but not predators, human or otherwise.

It usually took a lot of shaking and yelling for me to wake up, but not on this night. I opened my eyes and looked down at my mother lying on the bed in the corner of the room. I noticed that she had cuts on her thighs, and my calling out her name did not wake her. I sat in my bed screaming as loud as I could, "Help! Help! My muddah all cut up! Please hurry - I scared!" The space between the roof and walls where the tropical breezes flowed through allowed my cries for help to reach the neighbors.

Moments later, our neighbors came to the door, and I let them in. They found my mother unconscious and took her in a taxi to the hospital in the city. My siblings finally woke up. Afraid for ourselves and our mother, we found some solace by sleeping at our neighbor's house while waiting for my father to come home. Since his second job as a radio operator was on an oil barge, it took some time for the message to reach him.

It was early morning before father got home and took us to see our mother at the hospital. She was awake and happy to see us. She told us that someone had broken into the house and asked for money. When she refused, they threatened her and cut her thighs with a knife. Our life savings, a couple hundred dollars, was kept in a tin can way back in the corner under the bed. My mother embraced me and said, "Sheba, you save my life, and when you got up and started screaming, the thief run away."

I believe that some spiritual force whispered my name causing me to wake up, thereby saving my mother's life.

Cow Dung & Spirituality

One of my many chores growing up was to sit with a bucket under the rear end of my neighbor's cow and wait until enough dung filled the bucket. Sometimes, the placement of the bucket was not accurate enough to catch it all, and I would have to slip my bare hands into the hot steamy dung to ensure that the bucket was filled. The collected cow dung, mixed with dirt and water brought up from the river, allowed me to patch up the holes in the walls of our house. I would sit and wait with anticipation, hoping the cow and I could finish our business quickly, so I could be off to play with my friends.

Sitting on a log alone with the cow, my hand propping up my chin and my bare feet touching the earth, I would suddenly slip into that faraway place. My visions were of an open space with white and blue mists floating in different directions. Again, I would experience the feelings of warmth and love and a sense of belonging. I usually found myself back on the log with the sound of a "plop" in the bucket, or someone calling my name. I didn't want to return, and it would take a few minutes for me to feel fully present.

I felt a wonderful addiction to this other plane of existence. I found myself climbing to the top of the tree more often and even looking forward to staring at the rear end of the cow.

In those moments when our mind becomes still,
we can lift the veil to higher consciousness.

Poverty

The focus of our family was food and shelter. Our life was as simple as that in our village, and we all pitched in with the chores. Unaware of how poor we were, because there was not much in the village to have a comparison, we all helped each other as a family and community. I believe this one goal, simply to survive, helped keep prejudice and judgment away from the village. With no electricity, lamps lit the way in the evenings, and with a street pipe close by, buckets of water were brought home resting on top of my head. It would be a few years later that electricity would make its way to the village and turning on the radio and light switches would become a celebration in itself.

Our toilet was a hole in the ground sitting at the far end of the property with a makeshift shed over it. Old newspapers and a bucket of water served as our toilet paper. The distance to the latrine only became an issue once a month. Because we were exposed to parasites and other tropical health problems, my mother would have us all line up and spoon down some cod liver oil followed by some sugar to eliminate the putrid smell and taste. Five kids raced for the latrine! Some didn't make it all the way, but this routine eliminated everything from our bodies.

Food was supplied from the garden in our backyard, along with some of the animals we raised. A few items would be purchased at the rum shop or local street market. I still recall the first time I had to kill a chicken for dinner and prepare it. I was taught to say a prayer of thanks before killing it and place it in hot water; this made it easier to pluck the feathers. Every part of the chicken was used. To this day I struggle with any food waste.

Mother was our doctor. If we had a fever, she picked fever

grass and made a tea. Use of the small clinic in the next town was for real emergencies, like the time I jumped from the very top of a tree onto a broken glass and had to be stitched up without any medication. Strapping me down was the only way they could put a needle and thread in my foot.

Before walking to school, I fed the chickens, ducks, goats and our two dogs and fetched a bucket of water from the street pipe so Mom could wash the dishes. One morning, I had finished feeding all the animals except for Sefor, the female dog who was pregnant and nowhere to be found. I searched everywhere, calling out to her, and as I crept under our house, I saw her lying in a corner and could hear her whimpering. I moved closer and realized she was giving birth.

One after the other, six pups slid out, all covered with a mixture of blood and a gooey mess which Sefor licked off. I crouched down, hands propped under my chin for a close-up view. I was mesmerized by the process of new life and filled with a feeling that I was witnessing something amazing.

Just for a few seconds I had that same inner knowing that there was more to life. It was much bigger than that moment. It was the same feeling I had experienced when I peeked under the curtains that separated me from my mother and the neighbor who assisted her, as she gave birth to my sister. I had seen my mother cry and laugh at the same time. Abruptly I was awakened from my reverie as my mother yelled, "Hurry up or you go be late for school!"

On my way home from school, I ran through the sugar cane fields, my bare feet calloused enough to handle the rough terrain. I made it across the train tracks just in time,

22

as the gates closed and the steam engine gave a whistle. I had ridden that same train many times to visit my cousins. I wanted to check on Sefor and her pups. As I made my way to where Sefor had given birth, I could see her pups nursing, each one fighting for a spot. I felt like a spy as I watched in fascination.

Just then I heard my father's car pull into the yard and I ran out towards him, focused on getting to the treats he would bring from town before my siblings could have first pick. He drove his taxi in the town some days and always brought home a surprise for us, since we had no specialty stores in the village, except for the rum shop where they sold a handful of groceries and rum.

As my siblings and I fought over who got the most Chana (roasted garbanzo beans) that he had left on the car seat, I saw my father coming out from underneath the house with a burlap bag in his hands filled with something that was moving around. The bag was knotted at the top, and he walked quickly towards the river. When I saw Sefor standing in the yard, I knew what was about to happen.

I ran screaming after my father, "Please doh drown the pups! I go look after dem." But he kept walking towards the river banks without looking back and swung the bag into the water. I hated my father and shouted profanities, vowing never to speak to him again.

Blinded by my tears, I ran to the one place I could find solace, climbing to the top of the plum tree. I cried for the pups and Sefor, hoping the mixture of sadness and anger I felt would subside. I wanted to know why they had to die, but had no desire to ask my father. I must have stayed up in the tree for a long time, because all I remember was being called to dinner.

My awareness drifted back from the peaceful vastness that had somehow calmed my anger and relieved my sadness. Dinner was eaten in silence. Trying as hard as I could not to look, I could feel my father staring at me. With a softness in his voice, he said, "I am sorry, but we cyant afford to take care of de pups. It was a hard choice - we doh have enough for de family."

The joy in watching new life come into this world and the sadness, as it was taken away just as quickly, deepened my desire for knowing why life existed in the first place.

All experiences enrich our lives.

Family Photo, Trinidad

Life and Death

My exposure to life and death seemed normal in my
community. I was very close to my grandmother,
Mayo, who lived in a room within the family home. My
grandfather, whom we called Dada, lived with my cousins.
I was unaware of anyone getting a divorce or why they had
separated. It did not matter. My siblings and I enjoyed their
different personalities, and no one spoke of the situation.
Elders were taken care of by family members and respected
for their lifetime of experiences on earth. Their words of
wisdom were accepted with gratitude.

Mayo told many stories by the dim light of a lamp, making
it scary and intriguing. My younger brother and I always
wanted more. Right after dinner and chores, my brother
and I would knock on Grandma's door and ask if she had
another scary story. She always did. We huddled next to
each other, our feet curled up on top of the wooden bench,
afraid that a monster from her story might reach up through
the spaces on the floor and drag us into the night.

One day while I was recovering in the hospital from
appendix surgery, I was told that Grandma had passed away.
I would be able to see her at home in her coffin, since she
would be there for a couple of days for visitors to stop by
and pay their respects. That night as I slept, I could see her
in my dreams, and she smiled to let me know it was okay
and there was nothing to be sad about. When I got home
and looked at her in the coffin, she had that same smile on
her face, and my sadness dissipated. I could now celebrate
her passing along with everyone else.

Life and death slowly began to take on the same energy.
Dada, who rode his bicycle twice a week to visit, seemed
sad and did not say much. He would stoop near the mango

tree for hours, and I would stoop next to him, most of the time in silence. As a young girl, this practice taught me to listen to the quiet. You can learn a lot about someone by just sitting with them. I began to develop the ability to pick up subtleties. I wanted to learn to ride his bicycle. He gave his permission, along with a dime, so I could go to the street market on the other side of the village and buy my favorite dessert "jalabie," a sweet deep fried crust filled with honey.

The excitement and accomplishment I felt from conquering my fears of riding an adult bicycle were also shared by a grin and conversation with Dada. We now had a connection.

Grandfather...

You came to visit weekly.
Your bicycle your only form of transportation.
Khaki pants and white t-shirt
always adorned your skinny body.
An antiquated straw hat
shading your eyes from the hot sun.
Old leather sandals
showing off your un-manicured toes.

Black like tar and dry like leather
your skin exposed all those years
you worked in the cane fields.
A slight hunch on your back.
From bending day after day
to cut the sugar cane and load it up
onto the wooden bison carts
so, others could appease their sweet tooth and
men could have their rum.

When your wife passed on
you were never the same.
Words were barely spoken.
It's as though you left too.
A bottle in a brown bag
became your only companion.

Ignored by your family
harsh words used to describe
"the drunk lonely man."
They finally moved your bed
to the tiny room near the garage.
Confinement awakening your memories
Rum washing them away.

One morning they looked into your room
and saw you lying ever so still.
No speaking or shaking would move you.
Even their cries went unheard.

You came to visit weekly.
You taught me to ride your bicycle.
You relished in my joy
and smiled when I hugged you in gratitude.
I was the only one who could
penetrate your silence.
My laughter you said, "just like grandma's"
could set your spirit free.

Sometimes we can have a deeper connection
with others by just being.

My First Guide

The appearance of a floating figure at the end of my bed startled me. Although it was mostly cloudy and consisted of various colors, a quiet voice inside me said, "I am Jesus, your friend and guide." I remember not being afraid, but questioning the authenticity of the voice. I slipped back into a deep sleep and woke up the next morning thinking I had been dreaming. I was raised as a Catholic, my mother's choice, since that was the religion she and her family practiced. My father and his family practiced the Muslim faith. These two beautiful souls from very different backgrounds fell in love and raised five children in a community of varied cultures and beliefs.

My parents exposed our family to both religions, even joining in the festivities of the Hindus living in the village. I don't recall any discussions among our family or others in the community about religious beliefs. It seemed normal to join in any celebration in the village. The Catholic priest would come to our home around Christmas season, and everyone in our community would be invited to celebrate.

The Muslim Imam attended our yearly ritual of feeding folks who had less opportunity for food. I looked forward to this event. Grandpa would kill a goat, and mom would make dahl, rice and roti (Indian curry dishes). My job was to lay the banana leaves down on the floor in a circle - they served as plates for our guests. We ate food with our hands. I don't recall our family having many utensils. Most food was cooked immediately after purchase at the street market or from our garden, since we had no refrigeration. A stove made from clay and fastened to the ground outside was perfect for the use of our large iron pot.

I attended a Catholic convent for two years and was asked

by Sister Christina if I would consider becoming a nun. At twelve years old, I pondered this idea. This was also the first time I experienced any prejudice. I was now exposed to kids who came from wealthier families, mostly Indian and White, as well as kids who were from America and England. My mother had saved every penny she could to send me to the convent, hoping to provide me with a better education. But after two years of being called "Coolie" by the White kids, "Whitey" by the Indian kids and "poor girl from the village" by everyone, I convinced my mother to send me back to the village school.

Only one schoolmate ignored all the negative references made towards me and befriended me. She invited me to her home for lunch one day, and I was so excited when she offered me creamed canned peas - I had never seen this before. I was so overwhelmed that I cried tears of appreciation. It was the beginning of a lifetime lesson: to appreciate one good thing even when everything else seemed negative.

I also attended the local Hindu school for three years, attended the mosque with my father and participated in Ramadan, (a muslim ritual which included fasting). I would show off to my friends at the Hindu school that I was fasting and could not even swallow my spit. I was also the envy of my siblings, since dinner was first served to my father and me because we broke our fast around sunset.

I showed up for every celebration with the Hindu villagers. I especially enjoyed following the line of participants as they played tablas, danced and placed food near the river banks for the spirits. I was introduced to drumming, music and dance from the many Hindu celebrations which seemed to stir and awaken a spiritual force from within me.

I even witnessed a pundit sucking the negative spirit from a villager's big toe and nailing it to the wall. I appreciated the rituals from all the religions in my village. Some of the villagers believed in voodoo, and on many occasions, we would find a circle of salt in front of our door, which we had to step around or something evil would happen. My parents invited a priest and a pundit to bless our home.

We were told that someone had killed a rooster and buried it in our yard with the intention of causing us harm. These rituals did not seem to cause too much concern among the locals, as there was always a ritual that could wipe out the negative energy of any intent to cause harm.

Was the appearance of my first guide because of my Catholic faith? Why not a deity from the Muslim or Hindu faith? The presence of Jesus remains with me to this day, although I must add, our conversations are like two close friends confiding in each other.

We are never alone on this journey.

Premonition

One day when I was about twelve years old, I felt pulled by an inner voice to climb to the top of the plum tree. I sat in my usual spot and scanned the beautiful nature scene in my sight. I immediately found myself in that familiar space of warmth and love. There was no one else there, at least that I could tell, but an inner knowing of my family's and my future revealed itself.

I knew we would be moving to America and I would be married to a man with blonde hair and blue eyes. I also saw a young boy and girl who would become my children. It was like watching a television screen, and the current channel was showing a preview of my future.

Filled with excitement, I scaled down the tree and ran to my mother, tugging at her dress and shouting, "Ma - we going to America, and I go marry a man with blue eyes!" My mother gently rubbed the top of my head and said, "Okay, Sheba," continuing on with her chores. She sang all day long, some Hindu songs and my favorite, "Que Sera, Sera." Singing seemed to help her get through her daily chores.

The only other time I had seen blue eyes, except on some foreign students at the convent, was once when I peeked through a fence. This separated the village from the rich overseers who managed the sugar cane fields and the factory. There he was: a young boy playing near the fence, his eyes as blue as the sky and his skin almost pink. Our eyes met, and as he moved closer, I ran away, back home through the cane fields, for fear of being caught. We were poor village folks and had been told we should not speak to the rich folks who lived in the high-class community.

A few months later my parents spoke about moving to

England. It would be easier, since my mother still had her citizenship and the island of Trinidad was under British rule. My father was hesitant. All he knew was the life he lived in a small village, living off the land; besides, our family had little savings. My mother, however, being a strong fearless spirit, convinced my dad it would be best for us to move because the children would have more opportunity for a better education.

In Trinidad, unless we were straight A students, we would have had to work in the cane fields. My father was dedicated to his family and only wanted to see his children be successful in life. My parents decided to apply to both England and America. They were sure there would be no answer from the American government.

Change can be scary but it is inevitable,
if we choose growth.

Island Rhythm

Life continued as usual in our small village. We did our early morning chores and relaxed in hammocks at midday, when it was too hot for activity. After four o'clock, we slowly woke up to the chattering of neighbors or my mother directing us to the garden to pick some peas for our evening meal. This led to a bonfire in the village street, attended by most villagers. The elders told many stories here that held our attention and stimulated our imaginations.

Dancing around the fire was usually part of the ritual as the elders banged on buckets and bottles. I loved dancing and a variety of music. Every culture in the village performed in their own style. Everyone participated in Carnival, which closed down just about everything on the island once a year. Carnival consisted of rum, comradery and dancing in the streets to the sounds of steel drums. I would run down to the river banks where the old men carved out notes on used oil drums discarded by the overseers, transforming them into beautiful sounding musical instruments.

Saturday Mornings...

My bare feet hit the red dirt
in an exotic rhythm,
as I run quickly through
the sugar cane fields.
Lured by the sweet sounds
of the steel drums in the distance.

"It in she blood, man."
The villagers would say,
as I run past them along the dirt- road
toward the river banks
where the old men play their drums.

Out of breath with excitement.
I walk up to the fire
where the players are heating
and shaping their instruments
made from old oil drums.
Discarded by the overseers from the oil fields.

No words spoken but a welcoming smile
as I dance to the beat.
Feet shuffling, hips swaying.
Like some ancient ritual
seeping up from somewhere
deep inside my soul.

The old men know my routine.
They don't' mind giving me a dime for a dance.
As I move in perfect rhythm
my mouth watering, knowing
in a short time, my other passion
will be fulfilled.

It is Saturday morning.
The street market is opened.
The air is fragrant with the smells
of ground provisions, mangoes,
bananas, coconuts and sapodillas.
I go only for the honey- drenched pastry
that drips down my chin
As I devour every morsel.

Music and movement is universal.

Encounters in the Hammock

The heat of the midday sun and the quiet from the villagers resting in their hammocks made it easy to drift off into a deep state of relaxation. It was during these times, while gently swaying in the hammock and feeling the warm tropical breeze against my skin, that I would have many more experiences. Some of these experiences made me more aware of my physical body and the connection to the opposite sex. Boys were beginning to notice me. Theophilus, a heavy-set Black boy who lived near the train tracks, had a crush on me. He had a sweet disposition. He walked down the village street banging a drum, and as he approached my doorsteps, I could hear his singing, "Sheba, I love you and someday I go marry you."

All alone one day in the midday heat, as I swayed back and forth in a hammock, a young man from the village came and sat next to me. I was not alarmed because I already knew him and his family. He reached out his hand and offered me a beautiful large pink eraser, which was very impressive, because those were hard to come by in the village. However, the catch was I had to allow him to touch my breasts.

Because of all the religious lectures that drove the message home of the importance of remaining a virgin, I hesitated. He kept holding out his hand, and that pink eraser suddenly became the only thing I could think about. Just as I took the eraser and he reached out to touch my breast, my mother's voice penetrated the silence, "If you know wah good for you, go run as fast as you can and never come back." In a split second he was gone, and so was the eraser.

My mother reminded me to be aware of boys' intentions, and I drifted back to a daydream state, visualizing all the uses I could have had for that pink eraser and the envy of my friends.

The visionary vast space of blue and white mists would allow glimpses of shadowy figures in the background. I would always feel safe, but could never quite get enough of a visual to make any type of identification, except for one occasion.

As I arrived at my destination, floating and enjoying the loving energy, my guide appeared; this time I had an image. Jesus stood with arms wide open, inviting me in. Without hesitation, I melted into his embrace. In that moment, I understood that my journey on earth was just beginning, and my life would be interconnected with this space. As I embraced my guide, I noticed that my thoughts of him as a male shifted, and it was pure loving energy that existed, no longer categorized as male or female.

With this connection, I knew that the journey my family and I would make to another country would be quite a ride, but I was sure I would be protected and guided, no matter what.

Trust your intuition

Part 2

America - Our Arrival

In 1968, when I was fifteen, my mom, my four siblings and I stepped out of an airplane onto American soil at Miami International Airport. The contents of our suitcases, plus the $1,500 we had received for selling our home in Trinidad, were all we had to begin our lives in America. As we walked through the airport, I stayed very close to my mother and smiled at the travelers scurrying along. Smiling was a normal greeting on the island. My smiles were not reciprocated, and I even got some strange looks for smiling at everyone! I began crying and said to my mother, "I want to go home - no one here smiles at you." Always comforting, she said, "Give it some time Sheba."

My uneasiness was interrupted by my father as he walked eagerly towards us to pick us up and take us to our new home. We all embraced and cried with happiness; we had not seen our father for six months. In order for us to live in the United States, my father had been required to arrive before his family, prove to be a good citizen and have a solid job, showing that he could provide for us. Soon after that period, the rest of the family could officially enter the U.S.

My father worked as a car mechanic and had acquired an old car. We drove towards a very large bridge, on the way to the single motel room that would be our home, until we were settled. We had to stop in the long line along with other vehicles, as the bridge began to separate in the middle. I was fascinated and filled with curiosity and questions. How was this feat possible - could the bridge fall back on the boats as they passed through? I could not take my eyes away from this process of the bridge opening and closing.

It was sunset as we drove through the town, and the streetlights hanging on thick, electrical wire lit up the streets. My younger brother shouted, "Oh me God, moonlight 'pon wire!" Our laughter filled the air with feelings of adventure and discovery for me and my family. I felt like a newborn, experiencing life for the first time. This would be the beginning of many more new experiences.

Never take things for granted.

Our First Home

Nervous and excited, we arrived at the "Hotel Colon" on Flagler Street in downtown Miami. The frail looking man at the desk checked us in and seemed kind, but never smiled once. A single motel room for seven people did not matter. We had a flushing toilet and shower inside, and my father set up a small camping stove over the toilet for cooking our meals. As my mother and father got reacquainted, my siblings and I explored the motel and discovered fire escape ladders that lured us into climbing up and down.

It only took a few minutes for a tenant to run us off. Memories were stirred of the many occasions I was chased on the islands for stealing a neighbor's fruit or for peeking through holes in the wall at two grownups having sex.

That same fire escape would be the meeting place for my first love. Michael worked in his mother's clothing store, and on my way home from school, I would often stop inside and visualize what I would look like in some of the outfits. One day as I held up an outfit in front of the mirror, his eyes were looking directly into mine, and my heart melted. He asked for a date, and I explained that my father would never allow it. So he would show up at the bottom of the fire escape and play his guitar, singing me love songs. I was captivated by the romantic gestures and felt heartbroken when his family moved back to Brazil. This relationship set the tone for future loves, requiring poetry, love songs and romantic settings.

The next morning my father went off to work, and my mother took us to sign up for school. Later that afternoon, my mother walked into a store and asked for employment, willing to do any work. She was hired and would start the next week.

41

My First Sense of Spirit in America:

Awed by flushing toilets, bridges that opened-up, stores
where you could buy anything and restaurants that served
hamburgers and French fries, I had forgotten about my
spiritual journeys. The newness of everything made me feel
like a little child with a blank slate and stimulated all my
senses. Walking home from school one afternoon, I noticed
some bumps on my face and arms that began to itch. I
hurried to our hotel and entered the room, only to find the
rest of my family sprawled out all over the room.
Everyone had bumps all over their bodies, except for my
father. They were all making sounds of discomfort because
the outbreak was uncomfortable and itchy. We all had
chicken pox. We had only been in Miami for four weeks
and now we had to stay quarantined in our room.

It feels like hell, when you have a burning desire to scratch
and you are not allowed to touch because it could prolong
the outbreak. Lying on the floor on a mattress, bored and
uncomfortable, I drifted in and out of sleep. Suddenly,
I found myself once more in the vastness of white and
blue mists. My body felt light, and I was unaware of any
discomfort or need to scratch. I drifted into a deeper sleep,
and when I awoke, most of the itching had dissipated, and
some of the bumps were smaller. I felt an inner joy that I
had reconnected with my spiritual home.

Family in Miami Florida

Vulnerability in the Park

I missed my plum tree, the sugar cane fields and the ability to look out across the river. I was hungry to connect with nature. This seemed to be a portal that allowed me to journey to my spiritual home.

I began exploring my neighborhood and made my way to a park near the ocean. It was here that I felt some serenity as I sat under a palm tree and took in the expansiveness of the ocean and Miami Beach. I inhaled the fragrance from the many tropical flowers, allowing the warmth of the sun to gently caress my body. I became aware of the presence of someone standing in front of me. I looked up into azure-colored eyes that drew me in deeply. I remembered my vision of meeting a man with blue eyes, and I wondered if he might be the man from my vision.

Without much more than a warm greeting, I felt comfortable enough to follow this man to his motel room. I only knew he was a truck driver passing through. We sat on the edge of his bed, and he reached over to embrace me. As I closed my eyes, I could see the outline of a golden figure, and in a split second, my companion stood up and said, "You should go, and please be careful." I reluctantly walked out the door wondering: could he have been the one from my vision? As I made my way back through the park towards my family's motel room, I could feel a gentle energy at my back, and I knew I was safe.

My First Disappointment:

I was a newbie, only fifteen years on this earth and just a few months in a whole different country and culture. I was eager to make friends, hoping they would show me the ropes. Open, trusting and vulnerable, I experienced my

44

first disappointment when I invited my friends to my home and into my room. My parents had found a house for rent in Hialeah at a low cost and close to schools, and it was the first time I had a room of my own. After I had tried on various outfits, looking for approval as to which ones were in style, my friends decided I needed to pluck my eyebrows. They were too thick and met in the middle, apparently not the current style. They also suggested that wearing some makeup would make me more attractive. I was hesitant, because I had never done anything to my face except wash with water and soap. After all, any tomboy had to be ready, on the spur of the moment, for a new adventure.

With my eyebrows now separated and some lipstick on my lips, I looked in the mirror, unsure and uncomfortable. The approval of my friends brought me some excitement and confidence - I was now part of the group. Some time later, after everyone left, I cleaned up the clutter and discovered my favorite ring and outfit were missing.

My heart sank. The feelings of disappointment were overwhelming. I walked outside and sat under a small palm tree in our backyard, closing my eyes and wishing I were back home. Suddenly I felt like I was again at the top of my plum tree in Trinidad; I remembered that feeling of complete belonging and acceptance as serenity took the place of disappointment. I had found a place under the palm tree to connect. It was here that I would scribble many poems and writings that would earn me the position as my English teacher's special student.

A Stranger's Kindness:

In the two years we lived in Florida, there were many other situations where I could have been hurt, but I was always aware of a subtle energy at my back watching over me.

While I was waiting at a street corner for the light to change, a man's voice came from a car, and he pulled to the side of the curb asking for directions. We continued talking, and he seemed intrigued by my West Indian accent. He invited me to dinner, and I accepted, with some hesitation. I explained I had not been out to a nice restaurant and did not have an appropriate outfit. He smiled and said, "Get in the car. We are going shopping." The thought of a new outfit overpowered any feelings of reluctance, and in addition, I chose not to let my parents know of my plans.

We drove to a mall that had clothing shops and restaurants. I could choose any outfit I wanted. The idea that I could choose freely and not be concerned about money was foreign to me. I must have asked a dozen times, "Are you sure?" I found the perfect outfit and wanted to keep it on forever. I felt like Cinderella.

My new friend was fascinated with my excitement over a new dress and he could not stop smiling as we walked into a restaurant in the mall. As we waited for our meal, we had the opportunity to get acquainted, and he wanted to know everything about my journey to America. He told me he was an attorney from New York and would travel to Florida often. I did not even ask his age, because I was in the habit of connecting with people through their eyes and kind acts.

Our food arrived, and I stared at the steak on my plate until my companion inquired why I was not eating. Embarrassed, I explained I did not know how to use a knife and fork, because I ate with my hands in my village. Without hesitation, he demonstrated the process of using cutlery, delighted for the opportunity to teach me.

Most of the meal was spent discussing and perfecting my eating skills with utensils. As we walked back to his car, he stopped, took both my hands and said, "I want to thank you for letting me spend this time with you. I had taken so much for granted, and your gratefulness and excitement about simple things have given me a better appreciation for life."

He dropped me off at the same street corner and waved goodbye. A total stranger - an experience that could have been negative - was there some inner guidance as I looked in his eyes? Or was the subtle energy I felt through the whole experience my guardian angel? I was vulnerable.

Almost Kidnapped:

My mother had a part time job in Miami Beach at a fruit stand. Sometimes I would take the bus to visit her and check in after school, but mainly it was to acquire some of the delicious fruit. One afternoon as I stood waiting for the bus to return home, a car pulled up near me. The back door opened, and a man's hand reached out to pull me into the back seat. My mother's employer Gary must have been watching, because he quickly came to my rescue. Gary grabbed my other hand, still exposed outside the car, pulling me towards him and shouting obscenities at the men in the car.

Gary was a big man with a soft heart, and his presence scared the men. They sped off and disappeared within seconds. I was in a daze. It all happened so quickly, but Gary hugged me and said, "Lucky thing I looked over when I did. Not sure what it was, but something made me look. These men were trying to kidnap you." Was it luck or a guiding force that made him look in my direction?

Every experience is an opportunity for growth, find a balance between trusting and questioning.

The Séance

My family and I were slowly adjusting to our new life and wanted a little more living space. We found a dilapidated thirty-six-room home for sale on seven acres near the beach. My father worked as many jobs as he could, one of which was cleaning up the yard of this particular house. Everyone trusted my father; he was responsible and a good worker. The listing agent proposed that we move into the house for $100 a month and become the caretakers.

The history of this home was quite fascinating. At one time it had belonged to Spanish royalty, and after a family member died in the house, the rest of the family moved out. Over the years, it kept falling in and out of escrow with no interested buyers. It was on seven acres that went all the way down to the ocean, with a pool that had just enough dirty water in it to be home to a number of toads. The house surrounded a courtyard with a fountain in the center, and marble pillars supported the open ballroom. Thirty-six rooms in all! Only six were livable, but to my family, we were the luckiest people on earth. We moved in the following week.

There were stories going around the neighborhood that some family was now living in the haunted house. My school friends wanted to know if I had seen any ghosts, so I decided to invite them over to a séance. I chose not to tell them I had felt some energy roaming around in the large dining area and in the basement.

One day, shortly after sunset, my friends and I sat around an old large dining table with an antiquated chandelier hanging above. We turned out the lights, lit some candles and sat in silence until someone said, "Well, aren't we supposed to say something?" None of us knew the process, so I said, "We should close our eyes, and I will ask if there are any spirits here, to please show themselves."

Within seconds, a male and female could be heard, clearly arguing in Spanish, and then the candles blew out. Before I could ask questions, all my friends ran out the back door and were nowhere to be found.

The next day at school word had gotten out that I summoned spirits, and I was surrounded by my schoolmates, asking if my family would move out since the house was haunted. It was a subtle sensation, but I felt like a beacon for the spirit world and up to this point, I had not experienced any negative energy. We spent a couple years living in "our castle" until it was sold.

It is all about perception.
The physical and spiritual world are interconnected.

Georgia

My family and I enjoyed living in Miami, but missed the country environment. Once again, my mother was the one who suggested we move to Georgia, because she had heard someone talk about the green trees and beautiful spacious countryside. Mom and I took a Greyhound bus to search for a place to live. We had no destination in mind, so we got off the bus near a motel just outside Atlanta. It was near sundown, and it appeared to be a rest stop for the bus driver and all the passengers.

Hungry, my mother and I entered a coffee shop attached to the motel and were invited to sit at the table with the bus driver. Shortly after our meal, my mother and the driver got up, and Mom looked at me and said, "Wait here, I will be right back." I took her at her word, not thinking much about it. However, it seemed like a long time had passed, and I began to feel anxious, as my eyes welled up with tears. Just then a young man who had been sitting at a table across from me, came over and asked, "Are you okay miss?"

He had blonde hair and blue eyes; he looked thin and disheveled. Without hesitation I answered, "I am scared. My mother left me alone, and I don't know where she is." As he offered to sit with me, I could see a golden light shining around his head, and I knew I was safe. He sat next to me and gently held me as I cried. This was the first time I began to see colors around other people. I guess I thought it was normal, because it did not startle me.

Again, it was an inner knowing that I would be okay.

My mother returned and gave no explanation for her disappearance. Instead she said, "Come on, let's go." I simply thanked my companion and smiled at him as we walked away. The light I saw was like an unspoken language, confirming I was in a safe space. My mother asked if I knew that he was homeless and told me I needed to be more careful.

That day I realized my parents were not perfect. They were human beings having human experiences. "Homeless" was a new term, because in my village everyone looked after each other, and if someone needed food or shelter, it would be provided by the community. Kindness from anyone towards me or someone else always fills my heart with joy.

Don't jump to conclusions;
you could miss out on a learning moment.

Freedom and Prejudice

Mom and I found a nice apartment in a beautifully wooded neighborhood. We packed up the whole family and all our belongings and headed to Georgia. We stopped along the way, camping out and enjoying the journey. There was a feeling of freedom in picking up and moving and being able to start over again. This would never have been possible in my country of birth, since my parents were barely able to put food on the table. We were gypsies in a station wagon.

The year was 1969 when we settled in Georgia. I was in high school and my siblings in middle and elementary school. We connected with a few neighbors who made us feel welcome and enjoyed the spaciousness of the countryside.

My teenage years were in full swing, and the typical self-centered attitude caused some friction between my parents and me. I wanted to date; my father's over protective ways would not allow any freedom. After many attempts at sneaking out to meet with boys and being caught, having my freedom taken away as punishment caused more rebellious behavior. I had to get away from my father's authority. The apartment manager had already informed my parents that I was not allowed to wear my bikini by the pool because the wives were complaining that their husbands would stare at me.

I had a voluptuous figure, which I did not pay much attention to on the island because most women there were well-endowed. As soon as I arrived in America, I noticed both men and women staring at my chest. I felt some discomfort and began wearing clothes to hide my body. One night while everyone was asleep, I packed a small suitcase, crawled out the window and hitched a ride to my older girlfriend's apartment. I felt disconnected from my inner being and thought I had outsmarted my father - he would never find me.

The next day, as I lay by the pool with my friends, I looked up to see two men in suits standing over me. Without any hesitation, they asked my name and as soon as I acknowledged my identity, they took me to a juvenile detention center. It was here that I regained my senses: after spending a couple days with other kids who ran the gamut from being serious drug addicts, to attacking their parents, to stealing and being angry at the world. I knew I did not belong. I could never hit my parents and had no desire to let drugs take over my life.

I was never so happy to see my parents and promised not to run away. Their voices were gentle as they spoke of their fear of losing me and not knowing if I was safe. I could see things from their perspective. I snapped out of the teenage zone and reconnected with my parents, showing more compassion and empathy. Sometimes it takes an incident to scare and cause some fear in us, to snap us out of a negative space.

Because both my parents worked, I would help with my younger brothers and sister after school. One day my brother and sister, who were in elementary school, came home scared and crying. When I asked what had happened, they said a few kids at school bullied them, shouting that they should go home because they were niggers. My parents were appalled by the incident and immediately called the school. I am not sure what transpired.

Just a couple weeks later, my dad stopped at a grocery store on his way home from work and said someone had shouted at him "straight haired nigger." I could see the

54

disappointment on my parents' faces; we had not dealt with any prejudice in our village. Being from India, my father's family was very dark with straight hair. Folks in Georgia were not exposed to many Indians or people from other cultures. This was an era when Whites and Blacks did not see eye to eye. Some of the family dinner conversation alluded to us moving somewhere we did not have to deal with prejudice - but where?

Our family did not feel anger towards any one group, because, along with the derogatory comments from a few folks, we also had great friends and support from a variety of people. I was taught to assess people by their individual actions, a lesson I carried into adulthood.

I graduated from high school early because the English standard of education in Trinidad was a little more advanced. My dad would often talk to an attendant at the corner gas station where he filled up his car. He told him about our experiences and that we wanted to move. The attendant suggested we move to California. He lived out there part-time and was happy to help my family make some connections. He thought we would fit right in to a more eclectic environment. I spent my last couple months in Georgia focused on graduating and doing some dating. My father and I had reached an agreement. I was just about to turn seventeen, and the hormones were in full swing. We did not stay in Georgia long enough for me to find my place in nature.

See others as individuals on this journey of life,
not as a group.

California Here We Come

It was 1970 when my family and I arrived in California. We packed up our old station wagon and set out on another new adventure. Our friend recommended a motel in Venice that would allow the whole family to live in one large room. Once again we cooked over the toilet with our camp stove and slept on mattresses on the floor. I don't recall anyone in my family complaining. We were excited for the opportunity to explore new possibilities. My parents immediately found work, and my siblings went off to school. I worked wrapping packages at a local store to help my family. It was here that I met and became friends with a local boy who would help me get into college.

I am still always amazed, to this day, how the universe provides and guides us if we are open. This boy introduced us to his father, a soft-spoken man with kind eyes, who owned a rental home in the area. There was an immediate connection. He offered the family his rental home at a discount and my father a job as a gardener. The home provided us with more space and a more stable connection with the community.

Mother got a job just a block away at a hamburger joint. Even though clothes and sometimes food were donated to us by various church groups, we felt like this was really living. I attended the community college with the goal of becoming a therapist, but things were really heating up as far as my attraction to the opposite sex. So I dated quite a bit, even as I focused on school and took part-time jobs to help my family. The independent rebel in me surfaced, and I had no desire to be tied down to one relationship - which somehow seemed to make me more attractive to the opposite sex.

At 18 years old, I was allowed into night clubs. As I observed the other patrons, I noticed most of the females were loud and in many ways immature, whispering and gushing at the band members. All jockeying for position to see who would attract one of the performers. This behavior was foreign to me, since I was prepped during my younger years to be responsible and ready to raise a family. So, I sat back and observed. To my surprise, one by one, as the band members took a break, they came to my table and introduced themselves. My West Indian accent stirred curiosity and many questions about my background; however, it was the drummer who made it known he was attracted to me and asked me for a date.

When I saw his blue eyes and dark blonde hair, I wondered if he was the one I was supposed to meet. We made plans to get together and immediately felt a strong physical attraction, which overpowered any other insights that tried to surface. I fell into a sexual relationship that blocked my spiritual connection, or so it seemed. For the next year and a half, I spent my time in this deep physical relationship, hanging out in night clubs where my companion played. This was the early 70's and drugs, sex and rock-and-roll were on the agenda, which led to many hardships in our relationship. I was unaware of the negative aspects because I was too busy partaking and exploring this new path. I was having a great time and felt invincible.

For the first time in my life, I felt the need to cut some of my family ties and be free. When an opportunity came to go to Japan and work as a dancer with a band, I signed on the dotted line. I could always come back to college. When asked by the agent if I had danced before, I said yes. Of course, my family felt uneasy about my being so far away. I promised to send home every penny I earned to help out. All my expenses were covered, and my freedom meant more than the money. I loved my family dearly, but needed to make my own way. The winds of change were now flowing through my veins.

Dancing Wind...

I make the trees shudder on a cold winter's night.
The sand in the desert whirls in the heat of the sunlight.
I can whip the flicker of a fire into a frenzied flame,
Make the waves on the ocean swell into a torrid rain.

I make the trees sing a song of delight.
The sails on the boat puff up with a might.
The flower seeds are transported in my flight.
I can cool your skin on a hot summer's night.

Breathe in the sweet smells gently wafted your way.
Let the essence of my free spirit awaken in you today.
I am the dancing wind.

Dancing In Japan

In 1972 I was off to Japan after saying goodbye to friends, family and my male companion. My contract was for 2 months. Three other dancers and a small band were on the journey with me. The difference between us was that they all had some experience dancing. We arrived in Osaka, dropped off our luggage at the apartment we shared and went to the club where we would be performing. The manager welcomed our group and showed us around the club. I felt honored with so much bowing, especially, when I was addressed as "Annie San." There seemed to be a great love for Americans and their culture.

We familiarized ourselves with the dressing room and the entrance to the stage, and were then handed our costumes, which looked like they were from outer space. The short dresses were made of pink, glittery material and were packaged with a G-string and some pasties. I had no idea what they were until later, at the apartment, when I sat next to one of the girls, the friendliest of the bunch, and asked "What are we supposed to do with the almost invisible pieces of the costume?" She turned to me and asked if I had worn this type of costume before at other performances. It took a moment for me to respond, as tears welled up in my eyes. Then I confessed, "I have never done this before."

She stood up in shock and blurted many sentences, all joined together. All I heard was that I had signed a contract! If the agent and club manager knew, they would be very upset and send me home. She then put her arms on my shoulder and said, "Tonight, for our first performance, stand next to me. Take a shot of whiskey, do as I do and pretend you are dancing in your living room. Besides, you can't see the audience anyway because of the lights." Her advice worked, except that I took two shots of whiskey, and when the time came to strip away the dress, I felt at ease.

After that night, I became one of the popular dancers in the club with many patrons sending flowers and asking for dates. Some included famous musicians from the States. I even had a sumo wrestler send the manager to ask for a date. When I looked into the audience and saw the physical weight of this man I said, "There is no way! If he sat on me he would kill me." Very upset, the manager told me it is an honor to be asked out by a sumo wrestler, to which I responded, "I don't care."

On another evening after a performance, a famous singer sent his manager with a dozen roses to ask for a date, and I replied, "You tell your Mr. [X] if he wants to go out with me, he can ask for himself." He was attracted to my feisty independence and came backstage and asked me to dinner. I enjoyed his company. He invited me to his room, and this was when the energy shifted. He said he had to finish a meeting and would be back shortly. Then he threatened me that I could not leave his room or else one of his security guards would find me. His words were "you are mine." Those are fighting words for a rebellious young woman. As soon as he left, I made sure no security was around and bolted out the door, not stopping until I got into a taxi. I was scared, but it did not stop me from socializing. I attended parties, drank a lot, smoked some pot and explored Japan. I felt completely free. No parents, no rules.

One night after drinking and smoking in excess, around two o'clock in the morning, I decided to walk home through a dark alley, feeling numb and fearless. I suddenly felt that something was behind me. As I turned around, a ball of golden light faded in the distance, and I felt safe. I made it to the apartment and passed out.

I woke up the next morning groggy and tired, realizing I was alone, since my roommates had left for a tour of the countryside. As I drank some tea and began to feel the life force re-enter my body, I remembered the ball of light in the alley and pondered its appearance and the energy I felt at my back. It was a familiar feeling. Was I being protected from something more sinister?

I spent an extra month after my contract ended because I felt a deep desire to explore the spiritual side of the Japanese culture. I visited beautiful gardens and connected with nature; I felt the same comfortable feeling I had felt in the past.

I attended some of the religious/spiritual rituals of the local area. As I peeled away all the basic rules most religions seem to embrace, at the core level I observed a belief in something beyond our daily experiences - a Higher Power that we are all connected to, no matter which path we choose to follow. Trinidad, America and Japan – with different cultures and religious beliefs - expressed similar desires – to connect with our higher consciousness – God.

Our connection with higher consciousness is within.

Coming Home

I rejoined my family back in California and was continually pursued by the drummer I had dated before my trip. Something was different within me; not only had I matured somewhat from my experiences, but I felt I had shifted to another level on my spiritual path. I could now see and feel spirit around me. I had a desire to explore many religions and thought of getting a college degree in religious studies. I was baptized in the Mormon religion, joined Nichiren Shoshu, a Buddhist religion, attended a Baptist church and others I can't recall. I was perplexed that each spoke out against each other when all I could see was one religion with the same wants and desires. This was when I adopted the word "spiritual," as opposed to "religious."

My boyfriend and I spent a lot of time together and shared an apartment. I worked odd jobs. After my short dancing career I kept some of my connections with other dancers. This led to an introduction into nude modelling. Once you set foot on a path it's almost inevitable you will continue down that path, until you remove the blindfold. It was easy money and even though I felt some discomfort I commited to a few jobs. I was hired by a child psychologist along with some other models for some still shots. He had us wear scary masks and pose in wheelchairs. We all thought this was a bit strange but he paid handsomely. I introduced my boyfriend to the psychologist. He began hanging out at the night clubs to listen to my boyfriend and his band perform.

We became close and he would say that we seemed happy and all he got to do when he went home was feed the cats. He later hired myself and another model to fly to Denver and take some shots of us in nurse's uniforms. He stated that this was all part of his work. One night blairing out of the radio as my boyfriend drove to work: psychologist runs amock kills wife and daughter and tries to escape to Mexico. As he was being chased by the police he pulled over and shot himself in the head. They found his cats shot to death in the trunk. It was not until a few days later I realized the possibilities of being a victim. The FBI contacted me and during my interview with them they said "you are very lucky, did you know he shot his nurse in the head, her name was also Anne. She was looking at the photos he took of you."

The discomfort in my gut had become intense and I was able to see that going down this path was incongruent with my spiritual journey. I kept busy with night school, household duties and part time jobs, that did not include modelling or dancing. I needed to move forward in my life and focus. I knew my boyfriend had two kids living with their step-mother, and when he wanted them to spend some time with us, there was no hesitation on my part. We became a family over the next couple months as they visited on weekends.

About three months before my 21st birthday, I began to feel nauseated and sensed that something was different within my physical body. I felt I might be pregnant, even though I was on the pill and still had my periods. I called my doctor who said it was impossible, this was a one in a million chance, but I should come in for a check-up. My doctor's face was one of shock. "Well, this is a miracle. You are three months pregnant." The news was surprising to my companion, the father-to-be, as well as all my family and friends. All my partying, smoking cigarettes and drinking stopped in an instant. Without any outside encouragement, I knew this was important. There would be a soul coming into this plane of existence, and I would be his mother. Yes, I knew it was a male energy.

During my pregnancy, I did not experience much discomfort physically, even though I gained a lot of weight. The only negative energy I felt was the slow deterioration of my relationship with my baby's father. He played at a local nightclub with a very popular band which exposed him to alcohol, drugs and partying. Before I became pregnant, my partner and I both indulged in sex and drugs without thought, but now we were going to be responsible for a new soul. This led to his coming home very late, on many nights drunk, stoned and belligerent. When asked where he had been, his response was filled with profanities. After many arguments, his arrest for drunk driving and his resistance to any of my suggestions, I decided to take a break from the relationship. I felt insecure and did not trust my partner.

I moved to my parent's home and found some solace with my family around me. I had their love and support. Being away gave me the opportunity to reflect. I thought about the ups and downs in my relationship. When I was just a few months pregnant, my partner and I had slept on the floor of a room he had rented. This was where he began to teach music. During business hours, I worked as his secretary and helped him at the beginning of his business venture. Shortly thereafter, I found a one bedroom apartment near the beach that was affordable and we settled in.

Within a couple days of my leaving, my partner phoned my parents home every day, desperately trying to reconcile and promising to improve. Having a healthy baby was my only focus, so I moved back in. I also focused on the good times and laughter we shared. We were still on shaky ground, but my spiritual experiences expanded. Somehow I knew this new soul and I needed to be together in this relationship with his father because we had chosen the challenges ahead to help us learn and grow.

The struggles during birth that led to a C-section were all part of my own growth. It's amazing what a mother in labor will vocalize. After being in labor for many hours I screamed out," I don't want to have this baby!" The nurse responded, "You should have thought about that before." The baby's head was caught between my pelvic bones, and it felt as though my back had split open. I was maturing on the physical realm and slowly shedding any blocks that kept me from my soul progression.

Every struggle, as a new mother and in my relationship with my partner, helped me continue to mature on every level. The doorway to Higher Consciousness was now a much larger portal, and the messages were much clearer. There were moments, especially after I meditated, that I could see that my partner was one of my teachers. I turned inward when I felt anger and frustration because of his actions and looked at my own lessons. Those who challenged me caused me to look deeper within myself.

Visting a Japanese community

Author with performers in Japan

Meditation and Guides

As a young mother, at age 21, I had to tap into my
childhood experiences of helping raise my younger brothers
and sister on the island. My mother and I grew closer, and
I depended on her guidance to raise my son, Ray. A couple
years later, my stepchildren had moved in permanently. So,
still in my twenties, I was raising teenagers and my young
son. At age three Ray displayed musical talent. He would
bang on items around the house, so we bought him a drum
set, and he quickly developed a sense of rhythm. He also
spent a lot of time building extravagant miniature town
models with his dad.

I continued waking up at nights and followed previous
messages to write. Short poems began to emerge. I just
wanted to go back to sleep, but new information was being
downloaded. I was guided to close my eyes and meditate.
Without any formal meditation teachings, I closed my eyes
and allowed all the thoughts flowing in and out of my mind
to occur without forcing them out.

I realized I must have been meditating all those years when
I connected with this peaceful space, especially when in
nature. I simply noticed my thoughts until they dissipated
and I entered a calm peaceful space. An image appeared of
a spirit who immediately announced himself as he sat under
a tree. He said he was one of my Earth guides and others
would reveal themselves when I was ready. I giggled, as
his appearance was that of an overweight Buddha, but his
joyous laughter sent a loud and clear message: I must never
lose my sense of humor.

All through my childhood, I had possessed the ability to
see the humor in most situations, which sometimes led
to punishment by the nuns. They taught at the convent

Ray

Lana

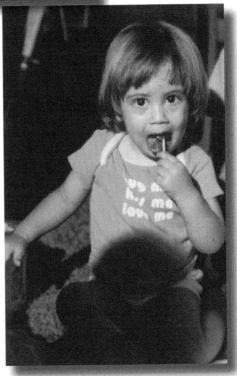

I attended for a couple years. The first time was when I giggled at the appearance of their habit, which looked like the flying nun, ready for take-off. I still could not stop laughing, even when I was made to stand in a corner and face a wall, right after a few smacks with a ruler. All my friends knew I could not control my laughter and that I would eventually pee my pants if I continued laughing. They usually egged me on.

I once laughed so hard I fell on top of a boy I was attracted to and peed as we were playing a game. He began laughing too. My laughter and smiles were infectious and easily caused others to find some lightheartedness within themselves.

There were times when my smiling caused some folks to be suspicious, such as a young man who was one of my teammates at a part-time job in California. We were focused on our project, and I sang as I worked. I looked over towards him and felt a discomfort in his energy as he looked at me. I smiled, and with a stoic look he said, "What are you up to? Why are you smiling?" My reaction was one of confusion, since I had never experienced that reaction on the islands. It caused me to question my sincere, natural response to other people, even those who appreciated my smiling and called me Smiley.

As my relationship with my partner grew more difficult and the challenges of being a new mother were many, my meditations also grew deeper. As my first Earth guide had said, many more guides were to reveal themselves.

They all represented some aspect of my own growth and served as a reminder of my inner core. A beautiful Indian female named Shanti represented peace in my life. A Native American male guide, a warrior called Running Water, represented the strong physical aspect of myself and my connection to Grandmother Earth. In my visions he was always running in nature. A much older Asian spirit who called himself Lao-Tzu led me to many wisdom teachings and reminded me of my connection with Jesus.

My son grew, and I matured. I began to realize I no longer felt the initial attraction towards my partner; instead it was replaced with hurt and anger. I could do nothing right. After cooking, cleaning and tending to our child and his two children when they visited, I would go to night classes at the local college. There was constant arguing and yelling between us, usually because he disapproved of something not done perfectly or because of my own anger at him for being out late at night. I began to experience slight depression because I felt trapped. He would often say that no one else would want me and that I would not survive just by smiling. I believed him. I was still stumbling to find my ground.

I always had hormone imbalances, bleeding excessively during periods or no periods for months. My feelings of unhappiness and depression affected my hormones so, this combination sent me into a downward spiral. I saw many doctors trying to sort things out. I communicated with my family that this downward phase had nothing to do with them and I would soon find my way back to good health and happiness.

I will never forget a group of five male doctors standing around me with one female doctor in the background, sharing what they thought was the answer to my ailment. They said all my tests were normal and they believe it was all in my mind. I could see the female doctor shaking her head as I took this all in. Deeply disappointed, because I knew something was wrong physically, I drove home and

70

laid on my bed. My first thoughts were that I was no longer capable of being a good mother. In the depth of my sorrow and feeling isolated I made a decision to end my life. I took a bunch of pills, hoping that my being gone would be much better for my family.

A family member came in after knocking on the door with no response. I was taken to the ER and had my stomach pumped. It was here that a nurse told me about a doctor who had been treating women for hormone imbalances, with great success. I saw him the very next day and even before doing any tests he assured me that it was not all in my mind. His recommendation was hormonal medication which gave me hope. I now wanted to live and be present for my family. Within a few days I began to feel happier and more balanced in my life. The big lesson for me, was to trust my intuition and not allow a diagnosis to determine my fate. I guess the Universe had more in store for me.

About five years went by with lots of ups and downs, both in my relationship with my partner and as a mother. But, as I grew through each experience on the physical plane, I also grew on the spiritual plane. I began noticing a parallel existence and that I could allow my awareness to travel to another dimension even as I went through my daily life experiences. I questioned my partner's love for me, but one day when he asked if I would marry him, I was elated and said yes. I thought this would make all the hurt go away and make things right. It did, for about a year. I felt loved and nurtured and smiled a lot more.

I had decided to study cosmetology at the local college and found my niche in stage makeup. This allowed me to do some part-time projects and still have quality time with my son. During the three months before my graduation, I began to feel a slight nausea, and my friends suggested

I might be pregnant. This seemed absurd, since I had stopped having a period for the past four years and was not ovulating. My doctor thought it might be because I did a lot of jogging. Exercise was one way for me to overcome any feelings of depression and unhappiness. I decided to see my doctor. He laughed as I suggested a pregnancy test, but did one to pacify me. A few days later the call came: I was three months pregnant. The impossible had happened once again, and I was filled with a deep inner knowing that a female soul had chosen to have a life experience with me.

My meditation that night took me into a large white spacious room. I was not aware of any other energy there, but was infused with the idea that we all choose to be together in our lives, on Earth, to learn and grow as souls. My son and daughter and I had made a pact before we reincarnated to be together. As difficult as it was to accept, I realized that my husband was part of the immediate group of souls that would all come together to learn through life's challenges. This was hard, but an important lesson.

My daughter Lana came into this world making her presence known. She screamed like an opera singer when she needed something and talked all the time as she grew, voicing her opinion. I knew immediately that the two very different personalities of my children would challenge me to learn and grow, or sometimes, I thought, run away from home.

My son's favorite response to any questions about his well-being was, "I am fine," but I knew it was not always true. He was just less verbally expressive. My daughter did not have to be asked, as she always let me know how she was feeling by communicating clearly. We were sure Lana would grow up to be a lawyer or perhaps an executive; her ability to hold her own in any argument or discussion was her gift. She was also very compassionate towards those in need. There were times we had fun and connected as a family, I thought it would be this way forever.

My sleep patterns had changed. Instead of sleeping through the night, I would suddenly wake up around 2 AM and not be able to go back to sleep. I would quietly go into the living room and sit on the couch so I would not awaken anyone else. Frustrated, I finally spoke out and said, "I need to go back to sleep." Immediately I experienced an inner knowing: "Just write and you will be able to sleep." I laughed and said, "I am not a writer. What am I supposed to write about?" - and the inner voice said, "Just write."

I began scribbling on a piece of paper and wrote a poem about my younger brother who had died in a car accident at age 21. Michael was a kind, compassionate human being and a free spirit. Then I fell back into a deep sleep. That night I dreamt that my brother was calling me. He appeared to be saving lots of people who were all walking up a hill towards him. I said, "I will sit on the fence for now and watch for a while." I continued to wake up at the same late hour every night and as soon as I wrote even just a couple lines, I could go back to sleep.

Over the next few years my children became my focus, followed by my pursuing part-time jobs as a makeup artist. This allowed me to drop my kids off at school before beginning my projects. It was important for me to hug them and wish them a great day. The unhappiness in my marriage had returned and so did the constant arguing. I wish I knew then the things I now know - how my children were affected by the yelling and negative energy in our home.

Leaving

One of the most difficult decisions I ever made was to leave my marriage. All the fears about making it on my own financially and the negative comments from my partner flooded my mind, especially when he said, "You think you can survive in the world with your smile?" I was concerned about uprooting my children from their home and father. Every single day that went by, I thought about how to tell him that we needed to fix things. I was concerned he would become very angry.

During the next four years, I would make suggestions, such as we should consider seeing a therapist. When he asked why, I said, "Because we need to become friends." He laughed and responded, "You are my wife. You can't be my friend." I knew then that nothing else I could say would help us to heal our marriage.

My demeanor became somber, and for the first time, I found it difficult to smile. I escaped into the world where I felt nurtured; my dreams and visions grew even stronger. One day, as I stepped out of the shower at the gym, I saw my husband's grandmother who had just died. She smiled and said, "I came to say goodbye, and you will be fine." Then she disappeared. I must have stood in the same spot for a few minutes with my mouth wide open.

On another occasion, as I was doing laundry in our apartment building, the owner, who had died a few months before, appeared and smiled at me, saying, "I just came to say goodbye." Entities began appearing, and it became overwhelming. I was bombarded with spiritual guidance, but also with entities who had some need or agenda. I did not understand and I began to feel fearful.

One of the positive things I remember from my relationship with my husband was when he saw I was too fearful to go to sleep. He asked what was wrong. After I explained about the overwhelming energies, he said, "All you need to do is say, 'This is my space and I am in charge!'" Desperate for sleep, I tested it out and had a good night's sleep.

Once my husband was asked to take some photos of a well-known medium for a magazine, and I went along. As soon as we entered her home, she took my arm. "You are meant to be a medium. I will mentor you." I responded that I would let her know. I felt afraid of allowing entities to enter my space and just was not ready to go down that path.

I had to take charge in the spirit world and in my own life. That message was clear. The physical and spiritual paths merged; one was a reflection of the other.

A close female friend who was aware of my situation suggested I accompany her to a party, which took much pleading on her part for me to finally agree. I walked in the front door with a sad, angry look on my face. A young man introduced himself and asked what I would like to drink. My response, "A straight shot of tequila." The tone of my voice made him ask if everything was okay. My immediate answer was, "You are barking up the wrong tree." He became more interested in me, even as I kept making stern, edgy comments that would normally make someone distance themselves. He kept prying and asking questions until I finally surrendered and poured my heart out.

It was the first time a man had listened so intently and made me feel heard. He was only 25 years old and a police officer, while I was 35, but our friendship grew over the next few months. We met at parks and the beach and spent most of our time talking and sharing. I finally had the friendship I longed for in my marriage and felt an attraction between us, but I made it clear that I was still married and had to reach some resolution.

One day on the spur of the moment, I told my husband I had met someone who listened and paid attention to my feelings. I truly wanted our marriage to heal and continue. It was the first time his response was gentle, he said he would try to be more attentive. I was hopeful and let my friend know I would be working on my marriage and could not see him anymore.

Over the next two months, my husband communicated and listened, and I felt a sense of hope. Then, slowly but surely, he returned to his harsh comments and demands. I slipped back into depression, except this time I knew there were other possible relationships out there where I would be heard. With assistance from my spiritual guides, I knew what I had to do.

I woke up one morning and before I could slip into a place of doubt, I blurted out, "We either need to go to therapy or separate so we can sort things out." My husband reacted with his usual loud, brash words as he responded, "We either stay married or get a divorce. There is no separation." I reacted by crying, feeling very emotional at his options. Somewhere from deep inside me a voice surfaced, and I said, "Then I guess we should get a divorce." His words became louder as he threatened to take my kids away from me, saying I would have to sign everything over to him. Of all the threats, the one that affected me the most was the prospect of losing my children.

I never once thought about "our stuff," only about the happiness and well-being of my children. That one thought of possibly losing my children permeated my mind, and

I felt sick and nauseated. I got in my car and drove to the supermarket where I asked a male friend to meet me. He was a kind, caring soul and agreed to help me. I vomited in the parking lot at the thought of losing my children. My life would be over if I did not have my kids. My friend arrived, and it was as though my guides spoke through him, because he promised to do whatever it took to help me and my children get on our feet.

I went back to our apartment, and said "Okay, let's get a divorce." Upon hearing those words, my husband immediately pulled me into his car and drove to his attorney's office threatening that if I did not sign everything over to him, he would make it difficult for me to see my kids. Overwhelmed with emotion, I signed without a second thought. I would get to be with my children.

He stated that my daughter could live with me full time, because she was too young for him to look after, and our son would live with him, but could visit me whenever he wanted. I agreed.

For the first few weeks my daughter and I slept on the floor of a girlfriend's apartment. My husband would only allow me to take a small couch and $1,500, which was money I had saved. I had no concern about "the stuff" - I only wanted my children to be happy. My every thought and breath were filled with the fear of survival, financially and emotionally. Would I be desired and loved? More importantly, I knew I had to do everything in my power to provide a safe space for my children.

After a couple weeks at my girlfriend's apartment, my male friend offered me a room at his brother's home, which I gladly accepted. Only at this time did I begin a romantic relationship with my friend. All I could see at the time was his caring and comforting during this rough scary period. I worked very hard and was able to get an apartment within a couple months. I began to feel an inner strength surfacing, but was not quite ready to be on my own, so I allowed my friend to move in. Our relationship lasted for about five years, and then I met and moved in with someone else. These relationships were like stepping stones that kept me from falling into the depths of my fears. This one lasted for four years.

I was turning forty five and had not been completely on my own for quite some time. I was scared. My fears began to fill most areas of my life, and I decided to study hypnotherapy, which became the most powerful tool in my tool box next to meditation. The director at the local YWCA allowed me to use some space in the building for a hair salon that provided services to members. I continued to freelance as a make-up artist. I also taught meditation and had a few hypnotherapy clients. I began to face some challenges and decided to take up scuba diving to overcome my fear of claustrophobia.

My first experience as I jumped off a boat into the ocean was complete nervousness. I found myself sitting at the bottom of the ocean, looking through a kelp forest and staring close up at a curious seal pup. As I looked up through the kelp and saw the sun streaming down, I noticed the peacefulness of just hearing my own breathing and nothing else. My fears were gone, and my connection with nature reclaimed. I felt a oneness with the seal, the kelp and the water. It was difficult to distinguish the difference between myself and my surroundings.

I would challenge myself whenever other fears surfaced and do the very things that caused discomfort. Sometimes it was one small step at a time. I learned to step outside my comfort zone and my world expanded.

Supporting others on a ropes course

Scuba...

Knowing I belong
I stand on the edge,
Feeling the weight of my equipment.
As I take a giant stride,
Anticipating your depth, your temperature,
Suddenly,
I am surrounded by your fluidity.
And just as quickly
I am pushed up to your surface.
Now I am ready
To penetrate into your mysteries.
Slowly I descend,
Feeling the weightlessness, feeling free.
Hearing only the sound of my slow deep breaths,
I am enticed to venture even deeper.
My whole being in harmony
With your beauty, your power.
We become one.
Knowing I belong,
I am free at last
From the coarseness of the world.

Diving in the tropics

Part 3

A visit to Trinidad

I had received my very first tax refund on my own and wanted to celebrate by taking my children to Trinidad to expose them to their roots. They both got a kick out of the local citizens' accents and seeing my village. Much had remained the same, and many folks I knew growing up were still there.

The fresh fruits and curried dishes served by some of my cousins were a hit. The experience that I believe had the greatest effect on all of us was when we walked down the village road and a voice shouted out, "Sheba, I go never forget that smile." Ms. Nen, a 95-year-old woman with missing teeth, ran out of her home to embrace me and my family. She had never forgotten my smiles. I cried with happiness realizing I had left something behind that no amount of money could buy.

Death in America:

My mother had recently died of cancer, and the journey to the islands reconnected me to my family, helping me to heal. My mother and I had our ups and downs, but always loved each other and enjoyed each other's company. I had lost a best friend. I spent a lot of time assisting my mother in her last few months at home.

The day before she died, I helped her into the wheelchair. As our eyes met, I asked, "You do love me, don't you Mom?" Her response permeated my whole being. "Always, Sheba, always." We had closure and a lasting bond. Somewhere deep inside I must have needed confirmation that I was loved. Even though I had experienced the death of my brother and understood that leaving the physical body was not the end, losing my mother was a hard pill to swallow.

I found some consolation from the priest who visited my mother during the progression of her cancer. He held my hand when I completely fell apart at the funeral. His caring and kindness sparked some energy between us. I was attracted to his passion and commitment to the Church, and he fell in love with me. We had only talked and embraced a few times, but the intense energy between us caused him to make a decision. He decided it would be best to move to a church far away. He was conflicted and felt he had to choose between me and the Church. Even though our connection was short-lived, I was grateful for the love that helped me through this time of grief. I felt that the universe had my back; whether in physical or spiritual form, I was always guided and supported. My mother appeared in many of my dreams always showing me that I was stronger than I knew.

Growing up

My children and I were all growing up. I felt ready to be completely on my own. My son graduated high school and moved with friends to Colorado. He became a talented musician and artist and was finding his own path. The first time I visited him, he picked me up from the airport and on the way to his home, which he shared with a friend, he said, "Mom, I am gay." My initial response was, "Are you sure?" Then I told him that nothing could ever change my love for him and I completely accepted his journey with his partner.

There has never been a moment when I did not love my children completely and deeply. My daughter, who was now 16 years old and becoming more independent, seemed excited that we would be on our own for the first time. She assisted me in choosing our apartment. The first pieces of furniture we acquired were her bedroom set, a couch and a coffee table. We settled in.

My daughter was now dating. I was feeling uncomfortable, but had no choice in the matter. She was maturing, and this was a new experience for me. It was a slow process for both of us, adjusting to this new path, but I began to feel some freedom from my fears.

Still concerned about surviving financially, I continued to work as a freelance makeup artist in the film industry, a meditation teacher and a hypnotherapist, working with many clients. I could now see auras and spirit guides around my clients. More importantly, I could see and feel who they were at a deep level, beyond the stories they told. I was determined to gain financial independence, so I wore many hats. I even attained my real estate license to add income to the pot.

One night, as I fell asleep on the couch, I woke up abruptly to a sweet smell that permeated my being, and I felt complete peace. I looked across the room and saw a shimmering golden light with a faded form. I asked, "Who are you?" An inner voice said, "I am Michael the Archangel - I have and will always protect you." The light disappeared. I sat up, taking deep breaths, hoping to fill my lungs with that sweet smell of peace, but to my dismay, I have never been able to replicate that exact experience. However, I knew my children and I would be okay. I was in my forties.

In the Middle...

Here I am.
In the middle of my life,
In deep reflection looking back.
Optimistic, uncertain, looking at the future.
Feeling so many things all at once – feeling.
Gathering the pieces to the puzzle.

Recalling every experience that allowed me to discover,
Wondering if I'll find the missing pieces,
There was a time when time seemed endless.
If I didn't get it done today,
I'd get it done tomorrow.

Now I find myself savoring every moment
And being in the moment of every experience.
Wondering- will I be desired just the same?
Recognizing the frailties of this human form.
Here I am,
In the middle of my life,
Heart-full
Mind-full
Realizing my reward.

Wisdom.

Awakened at night

Over the next couple years, it felt like a party in my bedroom at night. I would wake up, usually between two and four AM, with an entity standing at the foot of my bed, sending telepathic information such as, "Here is a message for a friend." Groggy and tired, I would respond that I just wanted to go back to sleep, but most of the spirits were insistent. I told them I needed to go back to sleep - "Please go away!" But the message was loud and clear. I could go back to sleep if I agreed to pass on the messages given. I reluctantly agreed and then was able to go back to sleep immediately.

The next day the message of the previous night was on my brain: "You must follow through." The thought of telling a friend that an entity had given me a message felt awkward. The next night I was awakened by the same entity standing with arms folded, "You agreed to pass on the message." I explained my dilemma, but the only words I heard inwardly were, "If you want to sleep, you must relay the message." "Okay, I promise this time I will do it." I saw my friend later that day and without hesitation I blurted out the message, waiting for a strange look or comment, such as, "Are you losing your mind?" Instead, the message was received with, "Thank you, that is what my priest used to tell me when I was a young man." I felt a weight lifted off me, and that night nothing interrupted my deep sleep.

I knew now that by following through with information from the spiritual world, I could sleep. A few weeks later, it was a different scenario. I would wake up to various patterns and luminescent colors floating in my room, sometimes with numbers inside some of the geometric shapes. As beautiful a sight as it was, I needed my sleep. So, one night in a half-awake state, I reached out my hand and said, "Please go away," then my thumb touched one of the luminescent patterns; it flew off into the corner of the room and disappeared.

Night after night, the same scenario occurred. Since I didn't get enough sleep, I sometimes took an afternoon nap, as time allowed. The first time I experienced my bed shaking, I thought it was an earthquake, because Southern California would often have small pressure releases within the many faults. I checked the news, but didn't find anything indicating an earthquake. As the shaking continued, I began to feel some concern and would ask friends or a close neighbor if I could take a nap on their couch. I was a bit hesitant, but had no choice, so I would explain my situation. Most responses were positive with very little questioning. There were no messages or visions, just shaking. My thinking mind needed to understand these incidents, so I began a search for help and information.

The people I spoke with had no feedback on my experiences, so I started looking on the Internet. This was early nineties, and the technology was not nearly as advanced as it is now. I came across a place in Virginia called The Robert Munroe Institute. One of the programs they offered included lots of meditation and quiet time, a few lectures by a remote viewer and meditation guide. No watches or clocks were allowed on the premises, and technology use was kept to a minimum.

A loud and clear message from deep within said this was the place for me, but when I called and asked about the pricing, I realized I would not be able to afford it. My first reaction was disappointment, and then I sat in meditation asking for some insight into my next move. The very next day, I received a call from the manager at the Institute who offered me the opportunity to come to the program free of charge, stating someone had cancelled and she felt a subtle guidance to invite me to the Institute. I was ecstatic and called my father to let him know. I was checking into flights and pricing to go to Virginia. A few minutes into our conversation my father said, "I would like to pay for your flight. You need to go."

Everything came together to allow me to attend the program. By this time, I no longer questioned the gifts. Instead, I sat quietly in gratitude for this wonderful energy and loving guidance that was always there when I listened.

The Monroe Institute

With great anticipation, I arrived at the Institute and immediately knew I was in the right place. For the first time, I was exposed to more than one person sharing his or her own spiritual journey, some different from and some similar to my own. We spent hours during the day in deep meditation in our own quiet space, guided gently by meta music and Mr. Munroe's voice. This allowed me to go even deeper. In the evening, we would gather as a group and share our experiences.

One of my many experiences was floating gently through space and becoming aware of an entity showing himself on a higher plane, appearing to be a physicist of some sort. He said he was working on helping us journey spiritually to other dimensions. Suddenly I noticed a wall in front of me and inwardly I asked, "Why can't I go on?" A knowing permeated my whole being: "You can move forward if you put on your crown." Then a golden crown appeared in my hand. My questioning, thinking mind took over, spewing out thoughts such as, "I do not deserve this crown. I am not perfect." The inner voice responded, "Well, if you want to move forward, you must put on your crown." My sense of adventure and curiosity to see what was behind the wall slowly led me to raise my hand and hesitantly, place the crown on my head.

Without warning, a large space opened, completely white like the clouds, and I was immersed in a feeling of pure, unconditional love and acceptance. The voice of a male/female energy said, "You must wear your crown. You are a child of mother/father god and you can break down the walls in your own life if you acknowledge your greatness." For me, this was very difficult to accept. I felt undeserving in my life and in the spirit world. One night as the group gathered to do our usual sharing, two different participants said they saw me in their dreams, one as an eagle ready for take-off and one as someone wearing a crown.

This was a surprise. I wondered if it were possible that we were meeting at a juncture or on another dimension, since we were in an awakening state and desiring spiritual growth. I returned from that experience elated, and it took some time before I could adjust back into my body. I still struggled with the idea of wearing a crown, but when I placed it on my head, I experienced more joy, clarity and confidence.

During the program, I even tried to recreate the same experience, reveling in the pure love I had felt, but it was never the same as that first encounter. The breath that permeated my whole being with a sweet smell and the immersion in unconditional love seemed like a one-time deal.

I believe you are taken to different levels on the spiritual path when you are ready. We are given deep reminders that we are one with God, and our consciousness is shifted each time to move us forward. I have since learned to let go of trying to re-experience these amazing fulfilling moments and instead commit more fully to my spiritual growth, knowing I will continue to have more of these special experiences.

Returning:

I returned from the Munroe Institute with more self-confidence in my life and a greater trust in the inner guidance that continued. Connections with like-minded folks and opportunities to attend programs were now available to me. The doors were wide open. I was drawn to attending sweat lodge ceremonies and working with Native American shamans. I felt a great connection with this culture, especially the idea that "all is connected." The references to the Earth as Grandmother and the Sky as Grandfather embedded a sense of sacredness in my mind.

Animals were also spirit guides. This whole concept helped me shift my awareness of spiritual connection from only being somewhere up above to being surrounded in nature by Spirit. The idea of above and below meshed into one, and I felt grounded. Over the years I taught meditation classes and helped others through my hypnotherapy work, but now I was drawn to helping clients experience their past lives and meet with their Spirit Guides.

After all, if a full circle was a way of looking at life on all dimensions, then at some point past meets future. However, I knew that being stuck in the past or focusing on the future kept folks from living in the present. Information from past lives and experiences were only for one's own learning and growth.

On one occasion, in a sweat lodge, I left my body, journeyed to a faraway place and felt myself perched on a cliff. I could see far off in the distance and at the same time close up in front of me. I, was an eagle. As soon as I noticed my transformation, a voice said, "You are Eagle Eye and you have the ability to see the big picture as well as the details."

This experience gave me more depth and insight as I worked with clients and on myself. I could see auras more clearly, and as they indicated any disharmony in my clients' lives, I could read between the lines. I had a close-up perspective while at the same time seeing the big picture and how they would be affected on their journey.

I tend to get comfortable with my space in the physical and spiritual worlds. On one occasion, within a deep meditation, an old man appeared in a boat, saying, "If you are ready, I will take you to the other side." I asked for his name and was told he was Charon.

I chuckled at the spelling and doubted my vision. A few days later at a newsstand I reached for a magazine called Parabola. I opened it to a page that spoke about Charon being the spirit that helps us cross over. I went home and that afternoon sat in meditation for a few hours hoping to have a deeper understanding of my experience. I was told it was time for me to shift my spiritual awareness to a higher level and Charon would assist me. I took his hand and let go of any hesitation, finding myself in a different space and being greeted by some new guides.

I enjoy the subtle ways in which information shows up to help us trust our experiences. It's like working muscles you want to develop. The more I helped others, the stronger my skills grew. I was now guided to do group sessions where everyone had an opportunity to become sensitive to energy and the spirit world. We practiced group healings on each other, and each person could describe whether they saw, heard or felt something. Through this process, individuals became empowered and began to trust their own intuition. I focused on helping clients download their inner experiences into the outer world where they could apply the information to assist them on their life's path.

Because energy is everywhere, connecting all dimensions, it is important to break down any blocks that make us feel a sense of separation. By expanding our awareness, we step out of the box and are empowered, knowing we have guidance at all levels.

Feeling Abandoned:

My father became ill, which required me to spend some time assisting him with doctors' appointments, cooking and paying bills. Because I was focused on helping him as well as getting my own life stuff accomplished, I did'nt think much about him dying. His health deteriorated, and he ended up in a coma. In the hospital where I slept many nights, I felt that he could still hear me. I would let him know it was okay to let go, that he would be with Mom, and his children would be fine.

He had always made it clear he wanted to die at home. As soon as we transferred his body to his favorite chair and all the kids were around, he took his last breath. It was then that I felt like an abandoned child. Both of my parents were gone, my siblings lived in different states and my own children had very busy lives of their own. My father's spirit must have felt my discomfort and he would appear often handing me a pink rose. This was a gesture that occurred each time I paid him a visit. He took pride in the one rose bush that produced beautiful pink roses. A pink rose was handed to me as I said goodbye each time.

The Universe is Listening

The Universe hears our every whisper of need and responds when we are ready. It was time for another round of life lessons. At one of my part time jobs as a mediator between employees and employers, I met someone who would become my next teacher and partner. I never had an image of what the perfect person or relationship would be like, but the Universe provided exactly what I needed to help me shift to the next level. I even dated a celebrity who wanted me to go off to sea with him to help with his cause and be by his side. He asked me to become his fiancé. I could never leave my children, and this relationship did not fit into my own journey. I was not aware of it at the time, but, I made so many choices that led to my present-day journey.

It's a good idea to stop and evaluate one's spiritual and physical progress. This process can gauge and guide you on your path. I had grown in leaps and bounds, but still lacked confidence and self-reliance. I also looked to the outside world to make me feel loved and needed at a very deep level. My new partner had a strong, passionate personality that challenged me to find my own ground and a sense of independence.

This was a harder road to climb. These lessons included revealing my core level issues, exposing years of my peeling away layers of life stuff. His words and actions did not provide an undying love. This was when I met Lao-Tzu again. In deep meditation, I entered a room that was simple, with an Asian décor and a coffee table right in the center. As I approached the table I could see a large wooden box and I heard a voice that said, "I am Lao-Tzu. Open the box. There is a gift for you." There was a green jade heart, and I held it in my hand, unsure of its meaning. Always in gratitude for my spiritual experiences, I returned from my vision of the room, my mind filled with the image of the jade heart.

One week later in my search for some meditation music, I entered a small store in the promenade. My eyes scanned the shelves and suddenly stopped: at the very bottom, all covered in dust, was my jade heart. I could hardly get the words out to ask the clerk how much. He said, "It has been here for a while so just make me an offer." I went home and held the heart in my hand as I meditated. I knew I had to be fully open to loving myself unconditionally, and then my relationships could be fulfilling.

Some of the experiences created by my interactions and participation in the journey with my new partner felt like a Mack truck coming at me full speed. Over time, as I dove in, instead of fighting, I could begin to see and experience myself as more confident and independent. The more I focused on my own journey, the more gentleness I noticed in my partner.

One day, in a moment of connection, my partner said, "I feel like you belong to the world and I am here as a platform of support so you can fly." This is our current relationship: a connection, a reason or purpose for being together - not "Romeo and Juliet," but with all the building blocks necessary for continued growth and self-realization for us both.

Be clear about your every want and desire because,
the universe will respond.

Grandchildren

My daughter had been married for a few years now and announced that she was pregnant. Lana had become a leader, with compassion and a desire to help those in need. The bond between my daughter and myself strengthened as she stepped into motherhood.

The moment I saw my first granddaughter I felt a new sense of love and belonging. My granddaughter and I had an immediate connection. When she was four years old, as we lay side by side looking into each other's eyes, my granddaughter asked, "Grandma, how come I know you?" I love that children are like a blank slate. They are not yet affected by earthly confinements, like duality and other experiences that slowly pull them away from the honesty and awareness they initially bring into this plane of existence.

I remembered a young boy I had once helped on a Team Building program. As we bantered back and forth, I said, "Oh well, youth is wasted on the young." Without hesitation, he replied, "Well, wisdom is wasted on the old." I have learned to listen to children intently.

As my granddaughter grew and her personality emerged, I could see so much of my mother's personality in her. My mother had died many years before and had shared a strong connection with my daughter. Perhaps, I thought, my mother's spirit had returned to assist my daughter on her journey. The unconditional love I have always felt for my children was now even stronger, and the bond with my granddaughter was sealed.

A couple years later, another beautiful granddaughter joined our family. She was a sweet soul, with a different energy that caused my heart to expand even more. As I watched her personality emerge, I could sense some aspects of my father who had died about eight years before. Some of my meditations were done with the intention of knowing if these two souls were once my parents who had now returned to complete their lessons and to help my daughter and her husband complete theirs.

The message that was downloaded showed that souls can be in groups and spend many lifetimes together in different roles, assisting each other with their own spiritual path. I observed the interactions between my grandchildren and family members and could begin to see how, as we challenge and love each other, it moves us forward on our path, if we are open. I enjoyed surrounding myself with my grandchildren's energy. I loved how they were in awe with new discoveries and filled with questions about everything.

Grandchildren...

I follow my arms down to my fingers.
Wrapped around your soft tiny hands.
As you tug and lead me with enthusiasm.
To see your new toy.

Your eyes filled with light.
Your words with excitement.
 You invite me to play.
"Come on Grammy, it's fun!"

I follow you down to the carpeted floor,
Not without a creaking in my knees
And sharp pains down my back.
For a moment, I am aware of my frailty.
Until the sound of your childish laughter
Envelops me, washing over me.
Like the healing waters of a baptism.

I engage in your story.
There is only this moment.

Mia & Briana

I was now hanging on tightly, as I rode the roller coaster of life. Always on the move, creating and implementing new ideas and making my physical body adhere to my adventurous desires, I was stopped in mid-stream. Over time, I noticed some swelling in my finger joints and discomfort in my feet. I thought if I ignored it and continued using my body in the way I had been accustomed, it would just go away. I was wrong; the pain grew more intense, and I finally surrendered to the idea of seeing a doctor. I will never forget that moment when he re-entered the room and said, "Well, it looks like you have both rheumatoid arthritis and osteoarthritis."

I had no idea how this would affect my life and said, "If I can hike and be in nature, I can handle anything." Even as a child, I was always moving my body and manipulating every muscle and joint to follow my commands. I learned that rheumatoid arthritis not only affected your joints, but was an immune system disorder that could attack your organs as well. As if that was not enough to swallow, my doctor recommended a type of medicine that might help keep my immune system from overacting and slow down the damage, but had negative side effects, possibly causing cancer. I did not wait for him to return to the examination room. Instead I ran out to my car, locked the doors and screamed at the top of my lungs, "WHY ME?"

Questioning:

Why me? After all, I exercised every day, ate healthy meals and meditated. I did not deserve this. I continued to work in outdoor education, helping kids and adults overcome fears, gain confidence and realize some of their life goals. One method used was a high ropes course which created physical and psychological challenges, where I was on the other end of the ropes supporting and guiding participants to succeed. I continued counseling clients through my hypnotherapy and meditation skills, always passionate about helping others. "If I ignore my diagnosis, it will go away." So I thought, but as a few months passed, it became clear: I would no longer be able physically to support others at work. I even noticed that it became harder to lift and play with my granddaughters. My denial was shattered, and awareness of my disability sent me into mixed emotions - from thinking, "Am I going to die from this or will it just go away?" - to depression.

The very things I helped others to overcome were now affecting me psychologically. This was a rare space for me, and I felt alone and afraid, as I curled up under a blanket on the couch. When my partner or anyone else asked about my well-being, I stated that I was fine. This is usually how I show myself to the outer world.

After a few days of wallowing in self-pity, I decided to meditate. My feelings of anger, resentment and "Why me?" prevented me from going within. I took some deep breaths, asking my body to relax and my mind to be still. Soon I had drifted off into familiar territory. Each time my thoughts went to "Why me," I took another breath that brought me back to a calm peaceful space.

I could now see an outline of a Golden Temple, and the more I let go, the closer it surrounded me. I could see there were four doorways: one at the front entry, one at the back that led to the next level of consciousness and one to the right and to the left, where souls passed through. It felt like a train station. I was aware of myself entering the Temple, and a voice said, "This is the Golden Temple of knowledge and wisdom - your spiritual hub."

Absorbed in all the details of this temple, I explored its many rooms. There was a crystal room for healing, a room where souls congregated and a library of sorts. In the large main entry room, there was Jesus, with Michael the Archangel at his right and Saint Germain at his left, forming a pyramid within the roundness of the Temple. An empowered female energy and shamanic healer stood at the center in the back, and behind her was a Council of Twelve, followed by three angels. This pattern validated many previous visions.

I found myself entering the crystal room, suspended in space with no support underneath my body, while light energies, in various colors, balanced my own chakras. I had an inner knowing that I could go the Temple anytime I needed. I could receive information for myself and others. I could also see the souls of some people I had known on Earth who had passed. I knew that my brother, father and mother had also passed through. This was a hub for some souls where they sort of checked in with a guide before moving on.

An awareness permeated my mind that I was capable of healing myself and empowering others to do the same. I was not alone. Then I found myself back on my couch, feeling empowered and supported. I had now shifted in consciousness to yet another level and met new guides. I could not wait to find out the role they would play in my spiritual journey and physical healing.

We are never alone.
Spiritual guidance is always there.
We just have to shift our awareness to that reality.

Journaling:

The roller coaster ride continued. One day I would forget the message and slip into self-pity and questioning; the next day my meditation would take me deeper into the Golden Temple, with the realization I had access to love, light and wisdom that would support the healing process. I decided to journal and every day I would give myself permission to write, whatever thought process came up.

At the top of a couple pages I wrote the words, "I am angry and do not deserve this." As I released my feelings on paper, I began to feel lighter and made space for things like acceptance. The more I wrote, the more freedom I felt, and the space for healing expanded. However, I still needed to know why, and as I sat with that one thought, a knowing welled up inside me. "It was the only way we could get you to slow down." Of course I argued, "Well, now I know and I promise to slow things down," but my spirit guides were not buying it.

Instead I was shown instances where I could have slowed down physically, but had not. I recalled that throughout my life I had constantly asked for assistance to walk my spiritual path, to learn and grow. The universe had listened and began creating gentle challenges to help me along, but when I continued to overburden my body and busy myself with things I thought were important, the challenges became stronger.

When I trusted universal guidance, growth occurred; when I ignored it, challenges arose. It was as simple as that. Information trickled in as to my physical healing, and it took about six months of journaling, meditating and researching R.A. to become clear about how to move forward. Against the wishes of my medical doctor, instead of taking the prescribed Western medication, I chose to eat organic foods and eliminate all grains, dairy, sugar and nightshades from my diet. Within a few weeks, I felt some relief from the pain. I understood that this would be my way of life, and my commitment to journaling, eating healthy, meditating and exercising would, holistically, help me find relief.

My New Guides

Being diligent with my diet and meditation and keeping up on research regarding strategies for healing found their place in my everyday life. I was excited to become more familiar with my newer guides. After asking for clarity in many meditations, I began to get some answers. I had spent many years communicating with Jesus, Michael the Archangel and the Council of Twelve, who all guided me through my challenges.

The beautiful empowered female guide said she was there to help me with my Reiki healing sessions and spiritual work. She showed me that I had the knowledge to heal myself and others. St. Germain repeatedly put a golden crown upon my head while sending the message, "I am the Violet Flame." In my meditations, I would see myself without the crown, and he would stick with the same ritual. When I finally accepted the crown as mine and repeated the words, "I am the Violet Flame," my body was filled with violet energy, and I felt elated.

Three angels had shown up early one morning as I was driving a long distance on the freeway. I became aware of them in the car with me. Startled, I asked my usual, "Who are you?" They replied, "We are the Three Angels." I had to know more, so I pulled off the freeway and Googled "the three angels." To my surprise, one site said that "three angels" show up before the second coming of Christ.

Was Jesus physically returning to Earth? Not too clear on what all this meant for me, I continued my journey with the Three Angels clearing the way. My next few meditations were of the Three Angels parting a veil that seemed to hang in mid-air, from the back of the Golden Temple. This allowed me to look at pure consciousness as far as I could see. I hesitated to pass through. What if this meant the end - my death? I just was not ready.

Every morning during my meditation, I would acknowledge my guides and make my way to the back of the Temple to see the Three Angels. Once again, they pointed the way and gently nudged me to let go and step off. After a few attempts, I finally surrendered and stepped out into pure consciousness. In a split second, I became one with the energy and knew this was a part of who "I Am." Jesus was not returning in a physical body; instead, there would be a "Christ Consciousness" awakening in all of us, if we were open. This would be a time for all of us to hone our spiritual skills, focus on our path and wear our crowns. We were moving into a Golden Age. Acceptance of this knowledge allowed me to return to the Golden Temple and experience the loving embrace of the Three Angels.

Over the next few weeks, especially in those moments when my body ached and I felt like there was no hope for complete healing, I noticed I was not connecting with pure consciousness or wearing my crown. My pain and discomfort overwhelmed my wisdom that I was so much more than what I was currently experiencing. As I gave in to the pain, I spiraled into a dark place of depression and a longing to shed my physical body. I wondered how I could be in this present state when I had been allowed to have such powerful experiences that connected me to pure consciousness.

The more I wallowed in this victim type of thinking, the more pain and depression surfaced. Why weren't my guides helping me? After all, I had traveled a long distance on my spiritual path and fully committed to more growth and wisdom. Then the answer became clear. I had focused so much energy on my pain and discomfort that I had forgotten to ask for guidance.

Lying on the couch, I closed my eyes and started chanting, "Please help me." I continued chanting to no avail. My eyes filled with tears. I surrendered to the idea of a lifetime of pain and possibly an early death. I shouted out with some angst, "Okay - I accept whatever happens!" Then I found myself standing in the Golden Temple of knowledge and wisdom. Jesus, Michael the Archangel, St. Germain, the Council of Twelve and other guides stood around me, all infusing me with feelings of love and peace, along with a message: "As long as you are in your physical body on Earth school, you will continue to learn and grow." There would be challenges, and each time I accepted these as opportunities for growth, instead of choosing resistance and self-pity, I would pass through to the next level of awareness and wisdom. A knowing permeated my whole being. I had guidance and love in the physical and spiritual world, but I did not apply it to myself. I had to send love to my pain and discomfort and give it a voice before I could have the one thing I needed most: self-love.

Acceptance, not resistance, makes us stronger.

I continued to ride the waves of joy and peace, pain and discomfort. Each time I took a deep breath and dove into the wave of no resistance, I came out on the other side with the ability to handle most situations, and the intensity lessened.

A particular childhood experience came to mind:

When I spent time in the tropical ocean with high, rough waves, I would jump as high as I could to get over them,

108

and I was always knocked down. One day after observing my ineffective strategy, my aunt said, "You know, Sheba, if you dive into the wave, you will come out on the other side." And I did! Now this memory has become my metaphor for the tough challenges.

I recalled many times in my life wondering why bad things happened to good people. These were folks who were positive, kind and thoughtful, hiding their discomfort, because that is what strong people did. Yet they suffered emotional and physical challenges. One day I sat down to write in my journal and before the usual thoughts flooded my mind, I wrote, "Why does life sometimes seem unfair?"

These are a few lines that were downloaded as I continued writing in my journal:

"It is all about perception. We all perceive situations according to our beliefs and life experiences. It does not mean it is so. Would things seem different if our life experiences, our beliefs were different? What if we could look at our outer world without judgment, put on the lens of acceptance of what is? The intensity of all our experiences would lessen, and we would pass through to the next level of consciousness, each time making it easier to ride the waves of life."

This too shall pass.

Fully back in my body, I realized the weight of this message. Like many others, I had lived in a two-dimensional world where things were black or white, good or bad, happy or sad, etc. When we experience energy moving through us, we gave it a word, a meaning. When it was bad, we traveled down the road of physical and emotional discomfort and when it was good, we tapped into the beliefs that we were familiar with and experienced joy. Whichever side we chose, we gave it power, and it became our reality.

Shifting from a lifetime of subjective beliefs to "I believe in nothing," as told to me by a shaman, was going to be a challenge. I had fears around the idea of believing in nothing. Immediately my mind wanted to stay secure by holding on to all the years of input. What would my life be like with an empty hard drive? From my previous experiences of taking deep breaths and surrendering to the moment, I expected to go through the usual steps of quieting my mind, relaxing my body and connecting with my guides to search for answers. Instead, I bypassed my familiar path and found myself floating out into pure consciousness, my mind empty of thoughts. I simply was. I felt my oneness with all. I became the observer without judgment or attachment. I was free.

I must have remained in that state of pure acceptance for a while, but when I returned, I understood the power of emptying my mind of old beliefs and judgments. Just as shedding old skin cells allows new cells to replace them, so it is that emptying our mind of old thoughts and beliefs leaves space for new ideas to take root. I am in awe of the power that we all have to help us transform our beliefs and shift our reality.

My life experiences would no longer have control over me. I would still have challenges. I would acknowledge and learn from the experiences, allowing them to pass through me with acceptance, simply observing as they dissipated. This was no easy task. After all, a lifetime of information was embedded in my mind's hard drive, and emptying it into the trash came with some hesitation. I was now ready to move from believing to knowing.

A Radiant Being

I was ready to shift to yet another level of knowing. It is true that the teacher shows up when we are ready. This can take any form - a person or spirit, a pet, a book or any number of things. My morning meditation took me through the Golden Temple and just outside, through the left doorway, I became aware of a radiant being cloaked in violet and I asked, "Who are you?" This female entity held what appeared to be a pen and paper in her hand. I could not help but focus on the pen and paper, since she kept reaching them out towards me. I knew they were meant for me, but was unsure of their purpose.

This was one of those times I wished communication between human and spirit was clear. It took a few meditations for that inner voice to surface, and I understood that I was given the opportunity to rewrite my life's script. Mixed feelings of excitement and doubt were fighting for space within my mind. "I get to change my life's script!" I felt honored, grateful and excited. Where would I begin? There were moments when I did not trust what I was seeing, but this radiant being was consistent and persistent. I felt like an artist with a blank canvas, having all the tools and ability to paint a new picture. I began by releasing old values and beliefs, but my guide erased that idea, letting me know that I could only create the positive things I wanted, from this moment forward, because they have already occurred.

No more attention to the past. I had already spent many years wallowing in guilt and asking for forgiveness. Now I had to let that go. I wrote, "I am now Anne 2.0. I now fully accept my crown that had been placed upon my head so many times, my work as a healer and teacher, me, as a part of all-encompassing God, connected to everything." With just those words, I felt a light expanding within me and extending far out into my aura. Words were spoken softly from my lips, "I am pure love, light and wisdom. I am one with all and all with one".

The most powerful words were "I am pure love." I was finally ready to own what I had been shown many times before, but felt there would be more information to be added to my life script. I could now begin to apply the new script I had created to my everyday existence. I wondered, "Why now?" I realized that I had experienced many trials and tribulations throughout my life, but by becoming aware of the lessons of each of those experiences, I continued to climb the ladder to higher consciousness in my everyday life.

I have to take responsibility for my life choices. I have the freedom and power to choose my path, and it is never too late to change my life script. I know that this is true for every human being. Everyone has the power and ability to change their life script. Does this mean I have graduated from life school?

Every challenge can be an opportunity for growth.

School's Out

The metaphor of life as school took root and branched out into many new pathways for learning. I noticed that my experiences and opportunities for growth had not happened all at once; there was a rhythm to them. I could now see clearly that I had never been given more than I could handle. It was my judgment and expectation of any life experience that made things seem overwhelming. There were times to focus and learn, and then came the testing to see if I learned my lessons. Now school was out: a break that gave me the opportunity to apply my knowledge, a time to celebrate with no challenges, a time to observe.

Everything has a rhythm.

There is one thing consistent in this universe: everything has a rhythm. During winter, some animals hibernate, and the trees shed their leaves; in the spring, there is new life. The ocean has its own rhythm, and so it is for us humans. We are a part of nature, and there is a rhythm that is within all of us. When we tune in and follow this flow, life is more effortless. When we override this natural system to fit into man-made rules, our life experiences become chaotic, and we feel imbalanced.

So how can we return to this flow and still be a part of society? Meditation is my number one choice, my go-to technique. It is the one time that we can become still enough to connect with our own rhythm and the natural world around us. The dance of life can be sweet. We may have to make some changes in order to live from this inner, effortless flow. Trust and keep re-creating your new life script. Make time to meditate. The more we practice, the stronger that inner muscle becomes and gives us the strength and ability to make necessary changes in our lives.

I believe my connection with nature as a young child was one of the reasons I could experience higher consciousness. With an absence of external stimuli, such as shopping malls and technology, more of my time was spent in nature, allowing me to be aware of a natural rhythm, the gentle, effortless flow that is at the core level of all life. When we peel away the layers of beliefs and judgments, we can expose the fundamental rhythm of life.

Connect with nature
and you connect with God.

My next step:

Now that I had shifted my consciousness to higher levels in a new phase of life, I wondered if my lessons were done. The message came back loud and clear, "As long as you are on earth school the lessons will continue." So they did, although not as intensely or as often as they had occurred throughout my life before.

My next step was to put into practice all the years of learning that came from my own pain and discomfort and from the people (my teachers) around me. When family, friends and people in general behaved in ways that caused me to feel upset or annoyed, I still found myself initially reacting with some harshness; however, it was not as intense and quickly dissipated. My new ability to step back and become the observer of any situation gave me more clarity and acceptance. When I came across people who challenged me, I perceived with new eyes, though sometimes it took every ounce of compassion and love to be in acceptance.

Each time I overcame any challenges, clarity and wisdom grew stronger. My inner muscles were developed, and I knew I now needed to share my knowledge and help others to find their own spiritual journey. The more I used my gifts such as Reiki, hypnotherapy, meditation and intuitive readings to help others, the more joy and peace permeated my being.

Anytime I have a rheumatoid flare-up or feel ill, all I need to do is work on someone else, allowing the healing energy of my guides to flow through me as I pass it on to the recipient. This is my go-to healing technique. I notice that when I ask for physical or emotional healing for myself, any discomfort will dissipate, but sometimes not completely. When I ask for light and love to flow through me to help someone else, the energy is much more powerful and lasts longer. It is better to give than to receive in my case. I feel like a catalyst, helping others find their light.

It is all about finding balance, that place where there is a natural flow between giving and receiving. I know it is important to take care of myself. Whenever I feel drained of energy because of too much giving, it is time for me to step back and re-access. As I continue to walk my path and integrate the lessons learned into my everyday life, things are less intense. My lessons are easier, and life seems more effortless. Sharing with others expands our own consciousness.

It is better to give than to receive.

Can't Escape on a UFO....

We can't escape on a UFO.
We must face the consequences down below.
We made our world what it is today.
We have even forgotten how to pray.

Wasting our resources, abusing Mother Nature,
Thinking only of today, oblivious to the future,
Now that our resources seem close to depletion,
With nowhere else to turn, we've come to the realization.
So we are looking up above with a gleam in our eyes,
Hoping to escape into the big blue skies.

We can't escape on a UFO.
We must face the consequences down below.

We react to the unknown through our fear,
Killing the wildlife that ventures near,
Building our homes in nature's path,
Calling the natural life flow a wrath.
Will we learn before it's too late?
Love is the only way to re-create.

We can't escape on a UFO.
We must face the consequences down below.
The secret to surviving is right here on Mother Earth.
Working together,
Loving one another
Shall be our re-birth.

Word!

Thoughts to Carry with You:

- The world is a mirror.

- A holistic approach, acknowledging body, mind and spirit, is the key to finding balance.

- Reality is all about perception, judgment and acceptance.

- Smile, you could completely change someone's life and create happiness in your own life.

- Have no regrets, as long as you learn and grow from your past experiences.

- Complete nirvana is not on this plane of existence - this is school.

- Life is simple. We complicate it by reacting from deep-rooted beliefs and experiences.

- Take a break from thinking too much: just be and notice.

- Dive into the heart of all your experiences, you will come out on the other side enriched.

- See others as individuals having a life experience; don't lump everyone into a group.

- You are an important part of this puzzle of life, so find your niche.

- Keep it simple: find a meditation that works for you, turn off the outside noise and listen to your higher self.

- Spend time alone in nature and truly connect. Sit under a tree, close your eyes and just feel the trunk on your back supporting you, just like your spine. Spread out your toes on the ground and feel connected, like the roots of the tree. Bring your awareness to your head and feel your energy being lifted upwards, toward the light and spaciousness of the sky, just like the crown of the tree. Nature can be your spiritual teacher.

- Be patient and forgiving of yourself and others; the richness is in the journey, not in the end result.

Coming full circle has allowed me to tap into a deep inner knowing that was already there from the beginning, and so it is for you.

Coming full circle reminds us that everything is connected. There is no beginning and no end...there just IS.

Conclusion

Through the ups and downs of my journey, I have learned:

- To be in gratitude for the opportunities to learn and grow.

- Not to frown upon those who challenge me, for they are truly my teachers.

- To transform any anger into love and appreciation.

I see that my biggest lessons have been to be more confident, to let go of my fears and to be willing to be uncomfortable in order to grow.

Most importantly, I have learned to love myself unconditionally.
(I'm still working on that!)

Mantra:

It is what it is.

By repeating, this many times over, even in the midst of chaos, we find that we can rise out of judgment and be in an empowering place of acceptance.

Our life experiences and our spiritual journey are interconnected. As we overcome life's challenges, we can shift to a higher level of spiritual knowledge and as we apply the information to our physical journey, our life challenges can lessen. We may still act out in the external world, but a deep inner knowing can give us understanding and acceptance of our reason for being, reminding us of the rhythm of life. Our paths and experiences may be different, but the internal rhythm of nature, which includes, us is the same.

Sometimes it is important to disconnect from the outer world and focus within ourselves. We all come into this world empowered with the ability to make our own life choices. Perspective becomes very important; our life experiences depend upon how we choose to see them. Is the glass half full or half empty? Are our experiences good or bad? I know this can be easier said than done, because we have a lifetime of experiences stored in our hard drive that influence how we react to our outer world.

The one solution I can pass on is to take one day at a time, or even each moment. When we are focused on what is in front of us, instead of being caught up in the past or living in the future, we have control over our reactions. It is easy, especially in today's world, to grasp onto so many beliefs and directions to find enlightenment, peace and happiness.

In the end, we can only find it within ourselves. We can learn from many different spiritual educators to help us find a path that resonates with our own individual journey, but we must always keep focused on and trust our own inner guidance. No matter who you are or where you live, it is the perfect place for you. Whether you were born with a silver spoon in your mouth or your hands in cow dung, your journey is important. Each person's growth affects the growth of this planet.

You Matter.

The sky never opened up,
but through every single experience in my life,
my heart opened up,
my awareness opened up and the universe opened up,
so I could see that nothing is separated.
We are truly one.

About the Author

Yasmine Anne Fernandez has over 30 years experience as a clinical hypnotherapist, meditation instructor, intuitive and energy reiki healer. Anne spent many years participating in the Native American culture and rituals. It was in a sweat lodge ceremony that she was given the name Eagle Eye. She has studied and practiced many concepts such as The Munroe Institute programs, shamanic rituals and with a variety of spiritual teachers.

Anne has worked and studied with renowned psychics Chuck Bergman and James Van Praagh. She has also worked with patients and doctors at many medical clinics.

She has a private practice, does intuitive readings and lectures.

Contact information:
www.changeyourthoughts.life
ionsanne@gmail.com

Made in the USA
San Bernardino, CA
18 September 2017